AT THE
END
OF THE
DAY

IMPROVING YOUR PERSONAL AND
PROFESSIONAL LIFE

RON   MUCHNICK   Ph.D.

PAGE PUBLISHING, INC.
New York, NY

First originally published by Page Publishing, Inc. 2018

ISBN 978-1-64350-985-3 (Paperback)
ISBN 978-1-64350-986-0 (Digital)

Printed in the United States of America

As we all know, and you have certainly been living it, life is a journey. I hope you enjoy the journey that the book describes. I hope it is fun & valuable.

Best wishes

Ron

Dedication

This book is dedicated to my parents, Ben and Rita Muchnick, who both certainly self-coached the concepts of loving, caring, and giving throughout their entire lives. *There are no better coaches!*

To Sherri, my wife and coaching partner for the past fifty-three years, and for all the years to come.

CONTENTS

ACKNOWLEDGMENTS

To the thousands of clients—both business and clinical—who have shown their ability to *self-coach* themselves through all kinds of problems and chaotic times. Without your hard work, creativity, and persistence, the SOLVE process would have remained just an idea.

INTRODUCTION

In today's world, personal coaches are an identified and accepted source in helping us attain a variety of life needs. Health and fitness coaches, nutritional coaches, home and personal coaches, to mention just a few, all provide us with guidance, direction, and problem resolution. The reason for these people entering our life is apparent. We don't have the time, energy, or alternative sources available to help us mentor and monitor our progress in attaining the personal goals we set for ourselves. We are overwhelmed, overextended, and overwrought with problems both at work and in our personal life, which restrict our ability to resolve existing issues before the next challenge is upon us. We are going 110mph in a 45mph speed zone, and something has got to give. Personal coaching provides one way to catch our breath and clearly think about what needs to be done, create options, develop plans to accomplish them, and then be able to put our plans into action.

At the End of the Day provides the availability of this same personal coaching process but allows *you* to be the coach. How in the world could this be accomplished? Well, let's not give away the ending in the very beginning. This is the journey you are about to begin and *At the End of the Day*, using the SOLVE process, will be your road map. Like any other trip you would be embarking on to a place you have never been, it is natural for you to be somewhat anxious, nervous, excited, and hopeful as to how it will work out. The best way to deal with these feeling is to get started. So, let us move forward and begin developing your ability to resolve personal and workplace issues . . . forever!

At the End of the Day, using the SOLVE process, is an exclusive, uniquely created five-step model that identifies a workable problem-solving system that will work in both your professional as well as your personal life. *At the End of the Day* identifies the ability that we, as individuals have, in finding and applying solutions to our life's problems. It is not just a book of hope; it is a book of *doing*.

It is one thing to want life to change for life to get better; it is quite another to make it happen. *At the End of the Day* is not designed to promote one-time improvement. The SOLVE process is not based on luck, and its success is not a fluke. Solutions to the problems you are now facing as you read these words are already there waiting to be discovered and be applied in the real world.

It is not that the SOLVE process will work on one problem and not another, on Tuesday and not Friday, instead the SOLVE process works—*period!* You need to understand that solutions will not appear by themselves. No way! You and the work, effort, and energy you invest in developing them will be directly correlated to your success. You control the dividends from your investment. You have the power to make things happen. At this time, you just do not know the process of how to get what you want to accomplish to happen. That is about to change. Forever!

INTRODUCTION

You are about to learn and most importantly understand the SOLVE process. *At the End of the Day* is a book that can be life-changing because when it becomes part of our life, it is a process that is then owned by its user. It is always available; and although energy, effort, and commitment are always needed, the SOLVE model remains ready to use for a lifetime.

The SOLVE model is a process that empowers individuals to be aware and understand the problems they face in a more productive way. They will not only be able to develop action plans, but most importantly will be able to self-initiate their plans into action.

From a business standpoint, the SOLVE model allows the individual to "process" their problems to a self-directed solution. This ability to *solve* one's own problems allows the organization's owners and management to deal with planning what comes next and how to get there, rather than getting bogged down in individual day to day problems. From a personal standpoint, being a SOLVE model individual builds self-esteem, confidence, and competency in knowing that we are capable of solving our problems by ourselves.

Also from a personal standpoint, *At the End of the Day* gives us personal empowerment in knowing that we can rely on ourselves for the answers to our continual problems. Knowing that by working through the SOLVE process, by following this problem-solving system, we will be able to deal with the issue at hand. With so much going on in our daily lives, it becomes difficult to "pull up" the ability to consistently deal with our problems. Being able to do so and knowing we have this ability immediately reduces the personal anxiety, pressure, and stress that we feel on an ongoing consistent basis.

I have spent a lengthy, thought-provoking amount of time developing what is felt to be a creative, productive, easy-to-use model that develops solutions to work-related and personal problems. The SOLVE model is a unique problem-solving process built on the foundation of being solution-focused rather than problem-focused. This process consists of developing an awareness of what it is that we want to resolve, creating plans to make it happen and finally executing those plans that result in experiencing the solution.

At the End of the Day identifies the assets, strengths, techniques, and skills we possess in overcoming problems, but somehow are overlooked when we become problem drenched. The goal of *At the End of the Day* is to have the SOLVE process become your personal problem-resolution system that is always available to use at your discretion. You have the power and control to develop solutions for the problems you experience. *At the End of the Day* allows *you* to promote successful change in your life.

CHAPTER 1

STATE THE PROBLEM SPECIFICALLY

Michael was not happy. There were too many things that were not going well in his life. He had just been passed over for the promotion he had wanted at work . . . again. He was not getting along with his boss who did not seem to appreciate his efforts. Michael was also having difficulty being accepted into the project group he had been assigned. And, oh yes, his relationship with Kim, his significant other, was beginning to head south. Too much, too overwhelming. Michael felt paralyzed and unable to deal with this accumulation of problems. He really felt like taking a very long nap, but he knew that would only compound his existing issues and problems.

Michael decided he needed some help. There certainly was not any available in the workplace. His company had just been right-sized for the third time. If Ajax Advertising got any "righter," there wouldn't be anyone left to even talk to. No, it had been made more than obvious that with this last restructuring, more and more responsibility for productive performance was going to fall directly on the individual employees.

The accountability for success or failure was now more than ever going to rest on the individual's self-directed shoulders. The days of having mentors and supervisors available to aid and assist in problem solving had been long gone at Ajax. A void had been created where help used to exist. If help is what Michael sought, Ajax was not the place to find it.

Well, if not at the workplace, then where else? Michael had recently seen some ads for finding life's answers through meditation and yoga. He had several friends who seemed to have a variety of people in their lives helping them. Steve had a life coach, Jessica had a personal trainer, and Josh had just hired a health and nutritional planner. It seemed as if everyone was attempting to seek out the help they needed to become a more successful and happier person.

Michael decided that this was what he was going to do as well. He would seek out those people who could make his life more of what he wanted it to be. He wanted to be more successful and productive in his job and finally begin to move up and ahead at Ajax. He just didn't think he knew how to get it done. He was ready to start a personal search, a journey, to find that person or persons that had the answers to his problems. At the end of the day, he wanted to own those solutions for himself. His journey was about to begin.

Since Michael was experiencing several troubling problems in his life, he decided that a life coach could be the answer. It certainly sounded like it was the tourniquet he needed to stop the bleeding. Wouldn't a life coach have the answers to why his life was becoming such a mess? The more he thought about this option, the more excited he became. He remembered that his friend Steve had a life coach. Maybe his coach could fix two lives at the same time. Michael called his friend and got the phone number of Marc Ifics, the life coach. Steve said to call him by his nickname Specs. Everyone did. Specs Ifics was going to save Michael's life.

Michael nervously dialed 1-800-ANSWERS and was connected to Specs. An appointment time was set for the following morning, and Michael could hardly sleep that night in anticipation that his life's problems would be resolved that very next morning.

At 8:00 AM, Michael arrived at Ifics's office. After a brief wait, he met the twenty-seven-year-old, well-dressed, and groomed Specs Ifics. Specs was a statement of details. His black framed glasses with the streaking silver trim seemed to define him. No wonder everyone called him Specs. His gray pants with his blue emblem embossed and red crested blazer with a matching red tie with specs of blue and gray randomly speckled through it made him seem matched to perfection. His white lapel carnation personified the statement that Specs Ifics was a man of detail.

As Michael entered his office, Specs asked, "So how was the drive over?"

"Fine," Michael replied and noticed that Specs began to show the beginning of a smile.

"What's going on at work?" Specs continued.

"Actually, it could be better. It could be a lot better," was Michael's response.

"Any special someone in your life, Michael?"

"Actually there is. Her name is Kim." Michael began to sigh. "She came into my life about a year ago, but the relationship has seen better days . . . and nights for that matter."

Specs then raised his right hand slightly and said, "I believe you have told me enough. I believe you have also told me nothing, although you think you have told me everything. Nothing you have said has been specific. I have no better of an idea about what is going on in your life since you answered my questions than I did before you answered them. Michael, in order to resolve problems, you need to state them specifically. You need to move out of the generic into the specific. You are talking too broadly not only to me but also to yourself. You need to give some specific thought as to how you will describe your issues so that not only I can understand them better, but that more importantly, you will be able to understand them better as well."

The Compass Concept

Specs went on to describe his compass concept. Michael definitely knew that getting lost in a problem was easy to do. He was living it.

"Michael," Specs said, "it is much more helpful and productive to have the problem defined in specific terms. Just going in a general direction will eventually ensure that you will become lost and misdirected. Being able to state the problem specifically, having a compass that identifies the specific direction you want to be taking, will allow you to move

toward your destination. It is critical that you
in a blizzard of problems. Knowing where you
what you want to accomplish needs to be a gi
as your first step of solution development allows you to begin
to identify the specific problem you want to solve."

Specs went on speaking. "Someone has to be accountable for providing resolutions to your problems. By the
process of elimination, that someone is you. But that is
the good news. That gives you the control in your life to
make what you want to happen, happen. We cannot control other people in our lives, but we can control ourselves.
For change to occur, *you* need to make it happen."

"Specs, you are absolutely right," Michael responded.
"I can't even tell you how many times I have been drawn
to issues that only bordered the real problem because it
was not stated and identified specifically enough. I have
felt that at best I was only achieving a Band-Aid effect to
the problem, and at worst, I would find myself chasing
smoke and putting out brush fires without ever identifying the real issues. All of this has always led to a great deal
of wasted time and a tremendous drain on my available
energy. In fact, now that I am thinking about it, this process always seems to move me to an increased feeling of
hopelessness and despair because I had been consciously
trying to resolve my problem and didn't. Since I was off target in my efforts, however, I would eventually discover that
I had failed . . . again. You know, Specs, it's going through
this process of futility that as an end result makes me feel
worse rather than better."

"This is why using specifics in stating your problem will act as our compass," Specs said, "and provide
the needed process to ensure you resolve your problems.

Identifying the problem specifically allows you to measure your journey and stay on course."

Going Grocery Shopping

"Think about this, Michael," Specs requested. "When was the last time you went into the grocery store just to pick up a few things? Sounds pretty vague, right? And what happened? Did you come out with a basket full of groceries? Did you see things that you just had to buy? Did you get diverted and distracted? Did you wind up getting what you needed? Did you remember what you went in to get in the first place?

"Michael, this is the same random process you are using when trying to resolve your problems. However, in order to get where you want to be, you need to specifically identify where you want to go. In order to solve your problems, you need to specifically identify what your problem is. Wanting to go on vacation is good. Winding up in Detroit when you really wanted to be in San Diego is not. Arriving in the wrong place when working to resolve your problems always leads to greater problems."

Michael looked thoughtfully at Specs and replied, "I am not appreciated at work. Now I can see that this is a vague statement and could mean many different things to different people. It is therefore absolutely necessary that 'not being appreciated' be defined appropriately and accurately. I need to know what is broken in order to fix it. Not being appreciated is a huge concept encompassing a variety of meanings and symptoms. Knowing what this looks like more specifically is going to be vital to the resolution."

Specs continued, "Michael, you need to understand that most of the time your problems need to be broken down into smaller identified pieces that then will become easier to work with. This is similar to making a specific 'shopping list' in order to identify your real problem. It is obviously easier and more productive to work with a concrete, precise complaint rather than a larger, overstated unmanageable complaint. This is why stating the problem specifically is such an important step.

Has Anyone Seen the Energizer Bunny?

"There is a factor that you need to be aware of Michael," Specs interjected. "You will discover that developing a specific statement of the problem takes energy. You will have to think and work at it in order to move from vagueness to specifics. To accomplish this, however, will take energy. Unfortunately, high energy levels and dealing with problems do not seem to be synonymous."

"You know, Specs," Michael thought out loud, "I have always thought that having a low energy level when trying to resolve problems was common. The feeling of being overwhelmed seems to expend my energy level in nonuseful ways. I begin to feel anxious, stressed, and feel the pressure of having an unresolved issue."

"The problem of dealing with the problem," Specs added, "is that it uses up your energy in nonproductive ways that could otherwise be available for problem resolution. It is due to this waste of energy that makes it important not to linger and languish with the problem for too long a period of time. You need to recognize that it will be necessary for you to be able to move on with your life, which means moving toward resolving the problem."

"You will find, Michael," Specs continued, "that nothing creates new energy and vitality more than being able to see a dim light at the end of the tunnel. Even a slight flicker will allow you to develop hope that an end is potentially in sight. It is this possibility that will then be able to be expanded to develop the reality of a solution. When the problem seems to keep going and going and going, your energy level will seem to abandon you. You will feel burned out. You need to recharge your personal batteries so that you can beat your drum to a new and different tempo. You need to develop a new rhythm, new marching orders leading to a different destination. In order to do so, it is imperative that you are able to see the potential solution. You will then be able to plug into the hope that lies ahead of you rather than the despair you are presently experiencing.

"It is not that you have to put the whole thing together at one time, no, that is not it at all," Specs added. "That will not happen, and in fact, you will never be energized if you wait for that to occur. Rather, it is the surge of energy that is associated with the understanding that you are now ready to begin to get out of your existing predicament you find yourself in. Hope, and with it energy, is on the way."

Michael could now see that the more specifically the problem was stated, the easier it would be to identify what needed to be done. Michael now thought it was this ability to "see" how to move forward that gave the energizer bunny his renewed charge to keep going and going and going.

Band-Aid Solution

Michael began to think he was truly onto something. He began to excitedly rub his hands together when he noticed a Band-Aid on his right index finger. "I see you have discovered your Band-Aid, Michael," Specs said smilingly.

"Band Aids. Hmmm," Specs thought out loud. "A concept to remember, Michael, is don't get too comfortable in using Band-Aids. One way to look at the Band-Aid effect might be to understand it as improving a symptom of the ailment, but not truly providing a cure to the disease. Short-term improvement might even result, but you will soon discover that your improvement is typically brief or non-existent."

Michael began to think of some of his friends who were taking a variety of medications. Taking medication, like an antidepressant, would help reduce the symptoms of depression, but until the real issues were identified in specific terms, a true solution would not take place.

"Look again at your Band-Aid," Specs suggested. "Band-Aids now come in all kinds of colors, designs, 'ouchless pads,' with or without mild cleansing medications, and a variety of other gimmicks. I can appreciate that all of these marketing efforts make you feel better about using Band-Aids. They look attractive and give temporary relief. It seems like you are doing something to help yourself and that you have taken care of your problem. Once you put on a Band-Aid, you stop finding other remedies because you believe you have taken care of 'it,' the problem. You have actually just put a Band-Aid over 'it,' and you are, for the moment, feeling better.

"But what is really going on underneath the Band-Aid? The infection is actually getting worse. It has yet to be fully treated and is festering. If you remain complacent with using Band-Aid solutions to your problems, you will eventually discover that there is a price to be paid for your neglecting proper treatment. If you never get to the real problem because you do not state it specifically enough, you can almost count on needing future problem resolving surgery."

Smoke Gets In Your Eyes

Just then, Michael heard the sirens of several fire engines. "Come over here, Michael," Specs said invitingly. "Look out the window with me. Do you see all of that smoke puffing into the sky?" Michael glanced toward the rising cloud of smoke. He wanted to continue to give more thought to Band-Aids and how they had become part of his life, but the billowing smoke seemed to divert him. He began to give this smoke issue more thought.

Spec broke into his thoughts by saying, "Just as the Band-Aid approach has been ineffective, Michael, the same holds true for the process of following smoke and putting out brush fires. I want you to think about the similarity that smoke has to the Band-Aids. It seems with both that something resembling problem resolution is taking place until the realization that only the fringe of the real issue has been touched. The specific problem, the forest fire, is still raging and the longer it takes you to get there, the more out of control your problems will become."

"You are right Specs," Michael said thoughtfully. "I have issues just like those in my life right now. It is hard to see clearly when my vision is smoke-filled. I think I'm proceeding in the direction I believe is the way out of danger, out of my problem. However, now that I am giving it more thought, I think that it would be in my best interest if I took a moment to look around at what is really going on."

"It can be difficult to consider that at the time you are dealing with your problems, you may not be using your best judgment," added Specs. "You might be willing to jump at a chance that appears to be a solution, only to find it is smoke. It only appears to be what you would want it to be, but in reality, it is not. Following the smoke can be enticing, and it certainly will keep you busy. It is, however, unproductive in solving the real problem."

"There will always be smoke to be followed in your daily life. In fact, your life appears to be regularly smoke-filled. It is not as though you cannot live in a smoke-filled room, it just is unhealthy and the longer you do, the more you put yourself at risk. It would be helpful if you began to question where the smoke is coming from. Is where you are going a brush fire, a remnant of the bigger fire, or is it the source? Unless you get to the source, the specific problem, one brush fire will only be replaced by another."

Michael began to give some thought to his workplace problems. Was there a smoke screen there? There had been several issues recently where Michael had arguments with various work team members. Michael had believed that a report had been started too late, that there was not equal help given on a project, and that not all of the team was attending team meetings regularly. There was enough smoke regarding these issues and others to choke a horse. As Michael gave this more thought, he began to realize that the source of the blaze that was spinning off these brush fires was that there was not an agreed to, unified position regarding team member responsibilities. Until this fire source was extinguished, until this problem was stated specifically, the smoke would continue to blind him. He needed to be the person to get to the source of the blaze.

Shall We Dance

"Take a moment, Michael," Specs melodically said, "to listen to the music that I have begun to pipe though my speaker system. See if you find it relaxing to go with the repetitive beat that creates the tempo of the music." When Michael had been feeling better and more confident in himself, he used to like to go dancing. His thoughts began to drift toward thinking about the dance he was now experiencing with his new partner, his problems.

"As you get into the music more and more, Michael, think about if it would be beneficial to view your continuing problems in relationships as a ritualistic dance. The dance consists of predictable patterns that are followed by each partner never varying from their identifiable sequence. This is the repetitive dance, Michael, of you and your problems. You can do this dance by now with your eyes shut. The problem with this dance is that it is being performed on the edge of a cliff and you continue to take the tumble. After you get up and wipe yourself off, you continue to follow the same beat of the problematic music over and over again.

"I hope, Michael, that you are coming to the realization that it is through the analyzing of these ritualistic, recurring dance steps that the specific problem can be identified. Taking the problem process step by step, it will become possible to identify what your work issue or other problem is, where it is coming from, how it happens, and its effect on you. You now know that you need to create a process that will change the rhythm of this ritualistic dance. The dance can no longer move in its predetermined way. Michael, you will need to initiate change. You will need to intervene by creating a new tempo, a new rhythm."

"It will be this process that you work to develop that will provide the change and create the new and different moves that will end this destructive, nonproductive dance. This is where your problem resolution will start and the beginning of developing an awareness of your problems getting better will take place. This is where you will bring in new innovative steps to change how the dance will now be performed."

Look Out Sherlock Holmes

"I feel like this is a mystery I am attempting to solve," Michael stated. There seems to be a lot of pieces out there, and my challenge is to put them together and solve the crime, solve my problems. So far, I seem to be a pretty good detective in seeking out the answers I have been searching for. Just like a good detective, I need to ask the right questions. In order to move away from describing my problems as though they could be anyone's problem, I need to answer several probing questions. By doing so, I will be able to move away from the general, vague descriptions that will not lead to resolving my problems."

Specs softly interjected, "Michael, I think you are beginning to recognize that you need to ask yourself specific questions. These would include questions like, when did your problem start? How often and where do they occur? What are the interactions that take place and who is involved? These questions will help provide you with useful focusing information. The more you are able to describe the complaint pattern in detail, the more meaningful your interventions and goals will be. As you begin to answer these questions that force out more detailed information, you will discover the value of a clear and specific problem definition in terms of actual behavior. Michael, you are about to discover that the description of these behaviors will open doors to new and different clues as to what your real problem is. In addition, Michael, you are about to begin to create options as to how you are going to go about solving your specifically stated problems."

Just as Perry Mason, Colombo, and yes, Sherlock Holmes always solved the problems they worked on, Michael thought he was now going to be able to join the ranks of these great problem-solving detectives. He must, however, continue to ask himself the probing questions that would put him on the right track. He needed to remember that he was not attempting to solve just any crime, any problem; he was attempting to resolve a specific crime, the specific problem that was negatively affecting his life. In order to do so, the "crime" needed to be stated specifically. Michael was becoming more convinced that being able to focus and identify what his real problem was by being able to describe it in clear, specific language would lead him to the solution of his problem.

Keep Your Eye on the Ball
Raising Your Problem-Solving Batting Average

Specs noticed a Padres baseball schedule sticking out of Michael's shirt pocket. "So you are a baseball fan, are you,

Michael?" Specs inquired. Michael had always loved baseball and still played on the Ajax softball team.

"What you are now becoming aware of is that by identifying persistent, repetitive, personal, and interpersonal behaviors, 'unsolvable' problems will become solvable. It is no longer that you cannot solve your problems, it is more of needing to identify specifically what is going on that is giving you the problem. The problem is more specifically describable than you might have previously believed it could be. It is similar to becoming a good hitter in baseball. Just because, Michael, you might be having trouble hitting the ball, does not mean that you cannot hit. It is more likely that at times you are not watching the ball leave the pitcher's hand and cross the plate. As you well know, learning how to hit in a different way is a more resolvable problem than not being able to hit a baseball at all."

"That same concept," Michael interjected, "probably holds true for my other love, cooking. The problem is not that I am unable to cook, it is more likely that at times, I do not know what seasonings to use or how long to cook the food I am preparing. This is again a more resolvable problem than not being able to cook at all or perceiving it that way."

Michael was coming to a realization that it was the use of the larger generic problem description, not being able to hit a baseball or knowing how to cook that resulted in lowering his percentage of successful problem solving. Michael was aware that as in all processes of change, a new and different awareness needs to be first developed and then skills and techniques, many of which are already available, need to be executed. Just as in baseball and cooking, he needed to practice in order to raise his average. The good news was that he could do it!

"Michael, I want you to remember," Specs stated, "that in order to raise your average, you need to overcome some messages and statements you are used to receiving. If you are having a bad day, or several, it does not mean you are a failure. If you are having difficulty handling work issues and stress, it does not mean you are a professional misfit. What it does mean is that you need to do some investigative questioning of your problem-related behaviors and figure out how to state your problems specifically, keeping your eyes on the ball all the way across the plate. If you then change your identified problematic behavior in some meaningful way, lo and behold, your average of success will start to climb. Problems will no longer keep you hopeless, and you will be able to move forward in your life."

At the End of the Day

Michael was pleased that he had begun to create a format that would allow him to develop his own specific problem statement in a simple yet effective manner. He needed to be aware of what was specifically bothering him. What was the specific problem? He then needed to go "grocery shopping" and make a specific list of what was happening in his life that was resulting in the problem he was now facing. This would certainly take some energy and effort, so he needed to be ready to be energized as he began the process.

Michael also remembered that he needed to forget the Band-Aids and put on some goggles to keep the smoke out of his eyes. He would also need to identify the "ritualistic dance" he had been doing. What was the vicious cycle that kept repeating itself? He would not forget to be a good problem-solving detective. It would be important for him to take some time to ask himself probing questions. He would remember that he was his own best witness to the "crime," the problem. Who was involved? When and where did it happen? What normally took place? How did it start and end? If he could answer these questions as they related to his problem, he would be able to develop a specific definition of what his problem was all about.

Lastly, he would need to be disciplined enough to keep his eyes on the ball all the way across the plate. It was important that he would not allow himself to drift back to vague, general statements of his problem. If he did, then he would have to try again and concentrate just a little harder. Michael knew that he was getting somewhere, but there was a lot to think about.

With that, Specs stood up, shook Michael's hand, and said, "When you have put your thoughts together in a more specific way, then call me and we can begin to work together. At this time you are not quite ready to do any more." He walked Michael to the door and specifically reminded him to be careful of the third and seventh steps of the staircase as they seemed to be more slippery than the others.

"Thanks for everything, Specs," Michael sincerely said, "I will work on your recommendations and set up a specific appointment for my return."

Michael took the next couple of days to think through all the new information he had just accumulated. He knew that he needed to be much more specific in identifying and working on his problems. He thought this would be a good time to rethink his problems. That had been made crystal clear.

Michael was not appreciated at work. My gosh, he had stayed late and worked hard. He remembered, however, what Ima Watchingu, his boss, had said.

"Michael," she said, "if you were more organized, you could cut your work time down by a third. Your working late just indicates how disheveled you really are."

Unappreciated? Well, maybe misunderstood. Michael had his way of working and seemingly Ima either did not understand it or she was totally unimpressed. Working late, putting in extra hours was definitely not appreciated. In fact, it defined Michael in a negative way. There, that was pretty specific. He was going to reevaluate this whole issue of time put in at work. Maybe it was time to reevaluate his organizational and time management skills as well.

Michael felt he was working in the right direction. His compass needle was starting to point in a new direction. This being specific was really helpful. The generic statement of being unappreciated did not help. This was better. He just had to work on it a little more. Boy, that Specs. He seemed to have 20/20 vision all right.

Another problem at work was that he was not being accepted by his work group team. "Wait a minute," Michael blurted out loud. "Not being accepted by my work group is not stated specifically enough. I can almost hear Specs groaning from here." Michael stopped to think about Specs and what he had learned. After a few minutes he began speaking in Spec's language.

Michael thoughtfully said to himself, "I have always thought that part of the problem is that there has not been an agreed to, unified position regarding team member responsibilities. Everyone seems to have different expectations. I certainly do of my team members, and boy, they seem to be continuously aggravated and frustrated at me for sure. So maybe that is why they are not accepting me. They don't like me. I expect too much from them without there being an understanding of what reasonable expectations look like. There is a definite need for a definition of specific responsibilities so that all team members can then be on the same page. Once these specifics are identified and defined, everyone can sign off on them and begin to feel like a team. We would be a team, working together to achieve a mutual goal with every member being accountable for what they needed to do. "Wow! Holy cow! I'll be darn," Michael exclaimed, "I think Specs would be proud of me on this one!"

Before Michael began to doze off, he wondered if specifics would help in his relationship with Kim. He thought about stating his Kim issues specifically. She had told Michael that he was not affectionate. Wait a minute, that was like being unappreciated at work. Nope, that was not a good enough, it was not a specific enough description of the problem. What did unaffectionate really mean? He would need to give this some thought. He would need to ask Kim what she meant, to be more specific. If he knew more about what she really wanted, maybe he could provide it. He wanted to. He loved Kim. "Hmmmm, specifics," Michael muttered out loud, "I certainly need more of them when it comes to Kim."

Although he was beginning to feel better about working on his issues, he still felt there was more that he needed to know. He had begun his journey; now it needed to be continued.

That morning, Michael had seen an ad in the daily paper about becoming a more successful person through meditation. He decided that this would be a great place to continue his search. He hurried to his recycling bin and found the paper and the ad he was seeking. Guru Seeka Ansura was offering five sessions for the price of four in his personal program entitled "I have the answer."

"What luck!" Michael said enthusiastically. "Just what I am looking for. At last, someone who could give me more of the answer I am seeking." Michael ran to the phone to make an appointment with the Guru.

Three hours later, Michael found himself sitting with his legs folded, garbed in a pure white satin robe with a white sash with the word *observe* stitched in purple roped twine all around it. Michael was listening more than intently to every word the guru uttered.

"Michael," the guru began, "it is not what is happening at this moment that is important. It is what is going to happen that we need to come in touch with so that we can focus on what will be happening to us next. We know the present, we are living it. We feel it because it is in the here and now. There is no need for explanations, only to decide if we are content and at peace. If so, there is little that needs to be done, and we may continue to enjoy the moment."

"If we are uncomfortable and not in sync and at ease with ourselves, then something must be done. That something, Michael, is to become focused on the future." What is it that you want to happen that is not happening? What would it look like if you no longer were experiencing this conflict within yourself? What would need to take place in order for you to observe the problem resolved? Michael, come in contact not only with your consciousness, but your subconscious and move to this place in the future where resolution and a quieter, more peaceful time has entered your life. Michael, move to that place and describe it. That is where you are going. Become comfortable with it because that is what you are about ready to create."

CHAPTER 2

OBSERVE THE PROBLEM RESOLVED

In the Beginning

Michael had come to believe that the process of change had to start somewhere. The guru had told Michael where that somewhere was. He said to Michael, "It begins when you are able to observe the problem resolved, when you are able to identify how you want your life to be rather than how it presently is. If all you live is the complaint, then all you know is the problem. Continuing to talk about and describe the problem reifies it, gives it a new, stronger, and more powerful existence. In doing so, we maintain exactly what we are trying to move away from, what we are trying to extinguish."

The guru's voice became more emphatic as he continued. "The more real and overwhelming the problem is made to be, the more likely the same thing, the same problem will continue to plague us. If you begin to believe that something else is possible, really believe it, then it becomes more likely that something different will actually take place. In order for this process to begin, however, you need to be able to describe what it is you want to be different. What will it be like when your problem is diminished or eliminated? How are you able to describe that difference? In the beginning, you may not be sure. That is why you need a guide. That is why I am here. Let us begin!"

The Miracle Question

The Guru Seeka Ansura had told Michael, "Asking a person who is experiencing a problem to think about a time when the problem is no longer present is asking a lot. We get so submerged in the problem, which then makes the problem bigger, that getting out of it would take a miracle. However, that is what solutions are all about, that is what needs to happen. A miracle needs to take place. In order for this to happen, the miracle question needs to be asked."

The guru looked directly into Michael's eyes and said, "This is the question you will need to think about and provide an answer. Pretend a miracle happened while you were sleeping, Michael, and you did not know the miracle had occurred. The miracle is that the problem that is troubling you is solved. Your life is better, more of the way you would want it to be. Now you wake up. How would you know the miracle had taken place? What would you notice about the people around you? How would they have changed? How would you be acting differently? What would you be doing? It is this description that identifies the miracle that needs to take place. Once you know what it looks like, you will need to follow the process and begin to live the miracle so that it becomes reality."

Pass the Clicker or Make a Wish

The guru asked Michael if he watched much TV. Michael did have a few favorite shows. Since Michael liked to watch TV, the guru suggested that he begin to think of his present dilemma as a TV show. He went on to say, "In today's world of the all-powerful 'TV Clicker,' it may be helpful to imagine yourself watching your problem-drenched life on TV. You, however, hold 'The Clicker' in your hand. Imagine clicking onto a different program that is about your life without the problem. How is this show different from the first? What do you see happening that changes this show and allows you to see yourself functioning without the problems you are presently enduring?"[1]

Wanting to make sure that Michael was going to connect with his concept, the guru asked him several additional questions. "Is it any easier to remember when you believed in magic and fantasy? Remember the tooth fairy, Santa Claus, and Tinker Bell? Try once again to see if there is still magic in the world and you are the magician. You have the power to tap your magic wand on your problems and they will disappear. After you have said, 'Abracadabra,' how does your life become different? How are you able to tell that the magic worked? What are you doing differently, and what are those around you doing differently? How would you describe this difference?"

[1]   deShazer, S. (1991). Putting difference to work. (pp.113,114). New York: W.W. Norton [MRA1]

Oh Yes, I'm the Great Pretender

Michael had always, as a child, liked to play "pretend." He would create a different place, a different perspective that removed him from his "real world" of the moment. He created a new reality, a different place to be. He had pretended to be up at bat in the seventh game of the World Series, in the bottom of the ninth inning, with the bases loaded, two outs, the scored tied one to one and the count three balls and two strikes. Whatever it was he was pretending, it seemed real at the time.

"It is time to pretend again," the guru stated. "This time however, Michael, you need to pretend that your problem situation has been solved. You need to pretend to be living as though your problem is really gone. Now that your problem no longer exists, what are you now pretending to do? You need to describe it. You need to hold on to this vision. You need to not let the pretend game be over. You are not that child any longer that has to stop pretending and come in for dinner. You need to hold on to your new view of life. Observe it. Do not let go of it. What you are pretending is the reality that you are about to create!"

Pass the Spot Remover

Certainly in his most recent past, Michael had thought that just getting off the spot he was on would seem to be an improvement in itself. "Have you ever been stuck in a place you did not want to be and that had become very uncomfortable?" the guru asked.

"You better believe it," Michael spontaneously replied. "It was like the time I had gone on a road trip and had car trouble. I was stuck in the middle of nowhere, definitely somewhere I did not want to be. That was when the repair shop informed me that it was going to "take a while" to fix my problem, and I was going to have to stay there longer than I expected. No fun! What a waste! A real bummer! Very overwhelming, frustrating, and depressing at best. That was when I wanted to say, "Get me out of here! Any place would be better than this."

"Michael, that is a great lesson to have learned," the guru responded. "The longer you stay in a problem-saturated position normally the worse life gets. When you stay there too long, it may seem as though you will never get out. Hopefully, you are beginning to realize that this is exactly the negative process that keeps you stuck in your problems. This is the type of situation, and they continuously come up in life, that you need to learn how to control and resolve.

"Being able to observe the problem resolved is the beginning of the process that creates a new awareness, a vision that there is hope, options, and different directions available that will help enable you to get out of where you are stuck. Just being able to identify these alternatives will begin to allow you to expect that you will get somewhere else that is different and better. This identification makes it more likely that you will in fact get there. Believing that you can get off your present spot is a great help in itself."

Let's Play Twenty Questions

Michael was discovering that the guru was correct. It was not easy for him as a problem-inflicted person to develop this needed futuristic, observable position. The guru asked

Michael, "Begin to think of some future directed questions to ask yourself that you think might prove to be helpful. Try to place yourself in the position of observing your problems resolved. Begin to make a list of your questions. Some you might want to consider are the following:

What will be different when you are feeling better?

What will be some signs that you are dealing with your problem in a more constructive way?

How will you know when things are going better?

What will significant others (spouse, friends, family, etc.) notice that will indicate to them that you are doing better?

What will be happening differently when life is going smoother?

The answers to these questions, Michael, will help make your observations a reality."

A Self-Fulfilling Prophecy

Michael now believed that if he wanted something to change in his life, he needed to be able to identify and describe it. The guru told Michael that statements like "It is amazing how lucky successful people are" indicate the involvement people have in being part of their own "luck-making" process. The guru said, "Michael, most things really do not just happen. We make them happen. You make things happen in your life. Even the lucky person who wins the lottery has to choose the numbers, buy the ticket, and claim the prize."

The guru continued, "In order for change in your life to occur, however, you need to be able to observe it, to visualize it, to 'see' it. When this vision is in your existence, within your awareness, it becomes something you can strive toward. You observe what you need to be doing to achieve your vision. This new awareness gives you direction, which allows you to fulfill what once began as a dream."

Brainstorming . . . Becoming a Visionary

Michael was getting it. He was discovering that it was this ability to observe the problem resolved that gave him the identification of the solution for his specific problem. Now was the time to become a visionary. It was important to "see" the solution and think about what was necessary to make his life better. This observation, this vision would identify that there were in fact solutions. He had just begun to identify that there really was a solution side to his problems. It was this process of visioning that allowed him to believe that solutions may in fact be attainable.

As though reading Michael's thoughts, the guru congratulated Michael on his progress. "I believe you are getting it, Michael. It is this beginning to vision, to brainstorm that will initiate your new beliefs. This change of vision will begin to challenge your existing belief system, which at this time is only problem oriented and excludes the possibility and potential of solutions. It is this initial change of perspective and change of vision that will allow you to begin to change gears. You will no longer be driven only by the problem. You will now actually see what solutions look like."

Give to the Needy . . . Doing a Needs Assessment

The Guru Seeka Ansura had been correct . . . again. That, however, was no longer surprising. Being a visionary certainly was a necessary step in observing the problem resolved. Michael did, however, want to make sure he identified the specific needs he wanted to fulfill. The process of observing the problem resolved did just that. The miracle question and visioning all led to developing a needs assessment. Michael then would be able to develop an identification of the needs that must be fulfilled in order to resolve his problems.

Michael was familiar with needs assessments from his work at Ajax. He had just never thought about doing one regarding his own personal needs in order to eliminate his problems. "My needs assessment should be simple, clear-cut, and productive, just like at work," Michael thought out loud. "In order to observe my problem resolved, there are several factors that I need to consider. First, where am I now? A specific awareness of what is going on in the present, what is problematic in my life at this time is necessary. This part of the assessment will be the easiest part to complete because I am living my problems daily. This is what I can and need to specifically describe. This is what I am experiencing and know. This is the first step in developing the needs assessment that is so critically important at this time.

"Once I complete this part," Michael continued, "I will need to identify what I want to happen rather than what is happening. This is where observing the problem resolved comes in. It will give me the picture of where I need to go and what is going to happen when I get there.

Now the goal I am striving to reach will become describable and, with that description, more real. The more specific, detailed, and enriched the description is the better the chances are of my attaining this future place as my reality. Without this description, there will be no place to go. There is only the reality I am living. There are no options or alternatives. Being able to observe the problem resolved will provide the direction for what is about to come next. Doing a needs assessment will really help."

The guru seemed pleased. He could tell Michael was progressing. Even though Michael was experienced in doing needs assessments, the guru wanted to make sure the importance of doing it completely and thoroughly was not missed. He said to Michael, "Remember, the final step, the purpose of your needs assessment, is to identify what you need to happen, the desired change, in moving from what is happening in the present to what you want to be happening in your future." The guru handed Michael a small worn strip of parchment paper. He instructed Michael to read what was inscribed. Michael read the following out loud, "The formula becomes: Future Desired Goal (-) Specific Existing Problem = Desired Change."

"By observing the problem resolved," the guru interjected, "the future desired goal, and knowing all too well the existing specific problem, you can identify what needs to happen in order to attain the desired change. It is the figuring out of this formula that identifies what is needed to make your goal a reality."

The guru added, "The point to be made at this time is that the change process continues or ends right here. Without observing the problem resolved, having a future vision, you are stuck with the problem and no place to go. Developing a needs-assessed future that reduces or eliminates the problem allows for the solution process to continue."

At the End of the Day

Michael thought this would be a good time to think through all that he had taken in from his experience with Guru Seeka Ansura. There had been so much, where would he start? Being able to identify that there were solutions to his problems and knowing what they looked like had been very helpful in his new solution process. Asking himself the miracle question, using his personal problem elimination clicker, wishing his problem away or pretending it was no longer present, had all been successful in creating a solution visual. Using any one or combination of these techniques had allowed Michael to "see" his problem-drenched life without his problems. What did it look like? How was he different, and how were the people around him different in response? Who needed to do what, where, and when to get Michael off the problem spot he was stuck on? Michael seemed to be asking himself the right questions in order to get the right answers in developing his problem-free vision.

The guru had also reminded Michael of a very important point that had been discovered. "Don't forget, Michael," the guru had said, "If all you can 'see' or talk about is what the problem looks like, then like a self-fulfilling prophecy the problem will continue to exist. Observing the problem resolved makes it possible that the problem may not have a place in your life after all. Since you are now able to believe that solutions do exist, the same prophecy begins to work for you rather than against you. Once you observe the problem resolved, it becomes identifiable as to what needs to happen in order for the problem to be eliminated. Fulfilling a needs assessment at this time can lead to successful change."

Michael's head became lighter. It was as though the guru's words made him sway back and forth. He lost himself in his future thoughts. Yes, he could envision, he could observe what his resolution would look like. Before he could totally embrace it, however, the guru had slapped his hands together in a forceful manner that broke Michael's concentration and observations. The guru mentioned to Michael that he needed to come back again to further embed these observations into his mind so that they could become the template, the compass for Michael's change.

"Besides" the guru continued, "you still have four sessions left. We don't want to get there too quickly, do we?"

Back to the real world, Michael thought. What a harsh reality. Well, Michael had gotten the idea. He had already experienced to some degree what the guru thought was the answer to his problems. The guru then moved toward Michael and bowed. Michael returned this gesture of respect and promised to revisit all that had taken place in their meeting.

The next thing Michael remembered was being home sprawled out in his favorite chair. There was so much to think about. Michael closed his eyes as he tried to create a peaceful place to think. So much information. He really wanted to move forward in resolving his issues. What would it look like at Ajax if his problems were resolved? He had never taken the time to think about that question. He had never been close to asking himself that question. That was quite an interesting question now that he was thinking about it.

He thought of the guru, and he immediately began to relax. Michael then began to experience the forming of a vision. It seemed like a movie set. Segments, pieces of his vision seemed to move into place, their place. It was like a puzzle that was coming together in chunks. There, there it was. He could see it. He could now make it out. He was at his desk. It was organized. There were baskets marked in and out. There were files that were clearly marked with project names and information. There was a sheet of paper with the heading "to-do" in bright red centered at the top. Numbers from 1–10 ran down the left side. The first numbers had tasks identified next to them and 1–4 had been scratched out. Ima was looking over his shoulder smiling. She was pointing to one of his project files, nodding her approval.

Wait a minute! The scene was changing. Michael was now walking into a team meeting. He was smiling and joking with Bill and Tami on the way in. Michael blinked several times, but no one disappeared. They were still there seemingly enjoying each other's company. Ima walked in behind them, put her coffee on a desk, and began asking each team member for their update on their committed part of the team's project. The reports that were being individually presented seemed to indicate that the direction of the project was that of moving toward completion. There were even mutually given compliments by various members of the group to one another.

So this is what it would look like when his problems were resolved, Michael thought. *Could this be possible?* Then he thought of Guru Seeka Ansura's echoing statement. "If you can vision it, you can create it." Well, Michael had the vision, he could see it; and boy, did he want to be living it. It all seemed so real.

Wait a minute! There was Kim. Scene 3, Take 1. Where did she come from? Of course, she was always there in his thoughts. Now she had materialized. Now this was a vision worth keeping! There was that special Kim smile. The vision seemed so natural, holding Kim's hand with her looking adoringly into Michael's eyes. All of a sudden, his vision was changing. Was Michael experiencing a case of double vision? The guru hadn't told him about these special effects. Wow, pretty cool!

There was Michael buying flowers for Kim choosing her favorite colors, blending them together, the shades of purple, pink, and magenta looking perfectly arranged. There he was again helping Kim cleaning up the kitchen. They were laughing, talking about their friends who had just left the party Kim and Michael had put together.

"Boy, was that party a lot of fun," he heard himself saying. What visions. He now knew what it looked like when he was living what he wanted to be living. Michael wanted to hold on to these visions forever.

For the next several days, Michael thought and thought about both Specs and the guru. He wanted the search to be over, but he needed to be confident that he had all the information and the process in place to solve his problems. Still not satisfied that Specs Ifics or the guru had provided him with all that he needed to know, Michael continued to seek out more answers. Certainly being able to describe his issues in very specific terms had to be important, but could that be all there was to it? Michael had found observing the problem resolved was in fact very helpful, but there had to be more. Would everything just fall into place as Specs and the guru had claimed?

The search for more answers needed to continue, Michael thought.

Michael wanted to know how someone could feel better about life, more optimistic about their future, have more confidence in themselves and still be confused as hell. That someone was Michael. He knew he was in the process of being able to handle his problems in a better way. He just didn't know where he was in the process. Was he in the beginning, the middle, or getting ready to wrap things up? His best guess was that there needed to be more to come. He respected everything Specs and the guru had provided him. He was also proud of his own self-discovery. Michael, however, was just not convinced that he had all the pieces to his puzzle. He needed to continue working. He needed to continue searching.

Three days after leaving the guru's office, Michael was listening to his favorite radio sports talk show. The ex-jock hosts were yelling per usual at the callers who were voicing their opinion regarding various topics. He then heard the Big Dog say that he would be right back to take more calls after a few interruptions from his sponsor. Then out of nowhere he heard this velvety smooth, baritone like, transfixing voice.

Michael seemed caught up in the velvety tone that was drawing him closer to the source of the words. He was now listening intently when he heard what he could not believe. The voice was asking him, Michael, if he had any problems that he wanted to make disappear. Were there any issues in his life that he seemed to be getting too use to living with? Were they getting to be like having dinner guests who stayed for a week after dinner was over?

"If so," the voice continued, "it was time to do something about them. Eliminate them from your life. Move to a different life place without leaving a forwarding address."

Wow, thought Michael, just what he wanted to do. Was he dreaming? Was he hallucinating? He actually pinched himself on his arm to make sure. When Michael said, "Ouch," in response to the immediate surge of pricking pain, he smiled. He was awake. This was real. He could hardly wait for the voice's next words.

"If this sounds like you, if I am describing your life, hope is a single phone call away. Call me, Mandrake at 1-800-647-2253. I don't use smoke and I don't use mirrors, but I do know how to make your problems disappear."

"Oh my gosh. Oh my gosh," was all Michael could shout. In his rush to grab his phone, Michael tripped over his couch and over a glass that he had left on his table. He didn't even hear the shattering as it hit his tile floor. "The number, the number," Michael was frantically crying out. "What was that number?" Through his momentary frenzy, he heard the voice answer his question. "The number to call is 1-800-647-2253. Again that is 1-800-MIRACLE."

Michael thought out loud, "Wow, I'll never forget that number again."

The phone was ringing, and after three agonizingly long rings, a voice answered, "Hello, this is Olga. How may I help you?" Michael introduced himself to Olga, Mandrake's assistant, and made an appointment for the very next day at 2:00. He thought he would never be able to wait that long, but it was the earliest time Mandrake had available.

It seemed like it had been twenty-eight days rather than twenty-eight hours, but there was Michael, waiting for Mandrake to open his door so that he might open his as well. He looked around the waiting room. There were five deco designed blue chairs and one orange. There were three yellow rose filled heart-shaped vases and one oval vase filled with red tulips. The floor was tiled in black glimmering marble with one lonely white tile set off to one side. His reading material consisted of seven months' worth of a magazine called *Black Magic*, and oh yes, there was one copy of *The Great Houdini*.

All of the hanging pictures seemed to be of the world's greatest magicians. There in the center of the room was Houdini with chains wrapped all over his body and his hands stretched out in front of him enclosed in gold-plated handcuffs. Off to the right was a lifelike portrait of Sigfred and Roy surrounded by two lions and two saber-toothed tigers. So lifelike, it was hard for Michael to break away from staring at them. Off to the right was a signed portrait of The Great Kreskin with a saw in hand cutting through a bright orange wooden box occupied at the moment by a beautiful young woman who seemed to be smiling through it all. Amazing!

His eyes wandered behind where Olga was sitting, and he noticed a picture of boats sailing on what appeared to be a quiet lake area. How different from the others. It did not seem to go with all the other pictures. Michael began to think about the entire room. There seemed to be exceptions to everything. The chairs, the flowers, the marble, the paintings—all had a piece that did not seem to go with the rest of the grouping. Exceptions! Michael found himself surrounded by exceptions. How interesting!

Suddenly, the door sprung open, and there stood the impressive Mandrake. Dressed all in black with the exception of a white silky bow tie, Mandrake certainly set the tone for dramatics. "Come in. Come in, Michael," Mandrake offered in a very friendly manner. "We have so much to talk about. I am anxious to get to know you." Mandrake invited Michael to sit in a chair that had the shape of a top hat next to a table that was in the shape of a rabbit with two long ears sticking up with light bulbs at the top of them. He pressed on the bunny's nose, and both ears immediately lit up giving off a comfortable lighted glow. Mandrake was now ready to get down to business.

3

LIST EXCEPTIONS

Back to the Future

Mandrake began by saying, "Olga has brought me up to date regarding the information you have provided her. It seems that you have already done some very good work in dealing with the problems in your life. That will give us a running start. By observing the problem resolved, Michael, you have begun to create a problem-reduced future that you are now able to observe and vision. Good, in fact, very good."

Mandrake leaned forward toward Michael and said, "I think you are now ready to discover the secret of how to go about creating that life you are determined to live. I am about to reveal to you the secret that will open new doors for a better, happier life. It is not really about magic but rather something that is magical. Michael, it is about . . . exceptions."

"It is not about what you see, it is about what you don't see, at least not at this moment. It is about exceptions. Oh, they are there right now. In fact, they are floating around in front of us as we speak. Can you see them, Michael? Of course not! Not just yet, anyway. And why is this? Because, Michael, you are not looking for them. They are not in your awareness, but they are already out there. They are already in existence. Our job is to make them appear. It will seem that they are coming out of nowhere, but they are really coming out of everywhere. You will need to do some personal work in order to make them materialize, but that is why you are here. To develop the skill and knowledge as to how to pull off this 'trick' whenever you care to. Not only will you amaze your friends with what will appear like magic, but more importantly, you will continue to amaze yourself. Michael, it is a breathtaking, exhilarating experience and soon you will know how it is done."

Michael was enthralled. He was leaning on every word Mandrake had uttered. He was somewhat spellbound when Mandrake continued, "You will need to begin to ask yourself new, different, and important questions. Has such a time already existed that you are presently searching for? Have you already experienced what you are now looking for? Do you already possess the strengths, assets, abilities, and techniques to resolve your problems? Are you just so overwhelmed with the problem that you don't recognize your own abilities? Or is it that you never recognized that you indeed had them in the first place? Did you come to believe your previous solutions, better times and outcomes were luck, or just happened, discounting your part in making them happen? Or will you be involved in a journey "Back to the Future" where you dis-cover that what you are searching for has already occurred?"

"Michael, remember in searching for problem excep-tions it does not matter if they happened ten days ago or ten years ago. The exception can be in contexts other than the exact one you are presently dealing with. In fact, this search for existing solutions, for exceptions to the problem, needs to be done on as broad a base of reference as possible. What is important is the identification of when things were better in your life, as you would now want them to be. It is therefore necessary to work at identifying and developing exceptions. However they are identified, they represent a time when the existing problem did not exist."

Overcoming Never . . . Remembering the Miracle

"Michael," Mandrake continued, "you know as well as I that asking yourself when you are deeply immersed in a problem when it was when you did not have the problem, will probably be met with an off-handed 'never' reply. That is certainly what it feels like, but that is not necessarily a factual or helpful reply. Identifying the last time when the problem was manageable is not easy. It is, however, neces-sary to identify the exceptions to the problem times. The miracle question identifies what you now want to happen. By remembering your own description of the miracle, you are often able to recall those times when you were living what you are now wanting. These exceptions then become a necessity in leading you to your next step of developing change."

Once You Know How to Ride a Bicycle

"So what I need to begin to do," Michael offered, "is to work at identifying and developing exceptions. These exceptions may have occurred very recently or I may need to do an extensive search over my past in order to identify them. However they are identified, it will certainly be reassuring and a confidence builder to know that I do in fact know how to solve my existing problems. If I was able to do what was necessary to eliminate the problem before, it certainly is hopeful that I can do it again. There is work to be done."

"That is correct, Michael," Mandrake responded. "You are now aware that paying close attention in detail to the period when you were able to deal with the problem in a successful way is a productive exercise," Mandrake reaffirmed. "Such positive behaviors, once they are recognized, form the basis for strengthening ourselves. When each exception is studied carefully, and who does what, when, where, and how is considered, it reveals a successful pattern. Since these are behaviors you have already mastered either recently or in past successes, it is certainly possible for you to replicate these exceptions again."

"So, it is kind of like my bike hanging on the hooks in my garage," Michael volunteered. "I may not have ridden my bike for a very long time, but now I recognize that once I know how to ride my bike I will always know how to ride my bike. Increasing the frequency of my existing success will be much easier than mastering new and different behaviors. Hmmmm . . . very interesting, Mandrake."

May the Power Be with You
It's All about Choices

Michael was beginning to reacquaint himself with regaining a feeling of personal power. Fortunately, he was beginning to believe that he had the power to solve the problems that were so overwhelming to him. Mandrake confirmed his thinking by saying, "Michael, you can figure out the solutions to your problems. It is not like you are going to need to learn rocket science, although it may feel like it, to get this done. What is most necessary, and is why the exceptions are so critical to problem solving success, is that you are able to make proper choices. It is the making of these choices that will lead to problem resolution. It is all about making choices, better choices.

"Once you identify times when you were making choices that worked, it then becomes possible to make these different type choices again, which will lead to problem resolution. It is not that what you want to happen cannot happen, it can, and it probably already has. What is going to be necessary is that the choices that allow what you want to happen will need to be made on a more continual, consistent basis. Making choices that consistently work in extending your problem exception frequency will certainly reduce or eliminate your problem."

Recognizing the Difference
That Makes a Difference

"Let me give you a hint of what will help you make the changes you desire," Mandrake added. "Once you begin to identify your exceptions, some real thought needs to be given as to what was happening at that time that was different in a better, more positive way. It doesn't end with just knowing that exceptions have occurred, this is where it begins. Now you need to get back to specifics, just as you did when you identified the importance of being as specific as possible when defining your problem. Defining the exception specifically allows you to discover how it came about and what you did to make it happen. Without this pinpointing process, it becomes too easy or natural to dismiss your part in the success. Rather than the exception just happening to you, it is important to identify how you made it happen.

"Claiming previous success becomes a critical part of successfully handling current problems. Identifying that you are not inept and at the mercy of your environment allows you to feel stronger and more confident in dealing with new and present issues. Nothing succeeds like success, so let's make sure you find some. Previous success, however, cannot just be wished for. It needs to be recognized as actually having taken place. You cannot fool yourself into believing something you don't believe. It needs to be real. Therein lies the importance of allowing yourself to believe. If you zip by exceptions and don't take time to smell the roses, then in your mind, in your belief, in your reality there are no roses. You need to take the time to review, to analyze, to reconstruct previous exceptions to your problems. Sound like work? It is, but the reward is developing solutions."

I Think I Better Think It Through Again

"I understand what you are saying," Michael said in somewhat of an amazed voice. "I am beginning to view my problems differently, thanks to my new ability to develop new truths, options, beliefs, and new realities. The original labels and descriptions of myself no longer make sense. If they were true then how could the exceptions have taken place? How could I be a failure, disorganized, incompetent, and still have the recognized successes, the exceptions I am able to identify. Now that the door to reexamining my problems is open, then I am required to ask myself if the problem is not totally me then what is the problem? This is a much better and healthier place to be. A whole new menu of problem identification begins to open up and new potential solutions begin to be constructed."

Mandrake added, "Once exceptions are identified, it is important that self-questioning begins. How do you account for your ability to having made the exception happen? What about you helped in being able to achieve this exception, this success? Are you surprised that you could handle the problem? Would others (spouse, friends, and relatives) be surprised that you succeeded? So what does this tell you about yourself? What is different about the times when this problem does not occur? What will have to happen for you to remain successful?

"Exceptions help us identify that our problem-managed future is real. Once success and difference in the form of exceptions is identified, it becomes more difficult to dismiss it. Once success is recognized our thoughts, beliefs, and actions begin to change. When this occurs, then the change process moves forward."

In summarizing his statements to Michael, Mandrake said, "Hopefully you are now aware that paying close attention in detail to the exceptions to your problem allows for the recognition of more productive, positive, and successful behaviors. When each exception is studied carefully and who does what, when, where, and how is considered, it reveals a successful pattern. Since these are behaviors you have already mastered, it becomes possible for you to replicate the exceptions to your problems. Increasing the period of existing success is much easier than mastering new and different behavior."

At the End of the Day

Michael was now beginning to understand how Mandrake had performed his trick of listing problem exceptions. It was nice to know that what he wanted to happen, his problems being resolved, had already happened. It was just difficult for him to believe it. Like magic tricks. Well, that is where listing exceptions came in. Sometimes he would have to look to the past in order to find what he wanted to happen in the future. He would need to take a few moments and think about times and situations when things were better, more as he would like them to be. Any time and any place would do. It might not have been for a long time, but as long as it happened, it counted. The trick now became to get back on the exception bicycle and ride it again. Do what he previously had done once again.

He would need to think about the different choices that he was making when his problems did not exist or were more tolerable. What was he doing that made a difference? Where did that difference go? What did he need to do to get it back? These more productive choices that provided the difference that worked better for him might be hiding in another context. The success might have occurred at work, or in his personal life, with friends, with

Kim, any and everywhere. It all counted. It was a success, and he needed to recognize it. He really had to work on this thinking part; it was not as easy as it may sound. It would take a real search for these existing solutions, these exceptions to his problem. He might need to identify how he was different at home and apply it to work or how he was different with his friends and apply it to his boss. The better and more thorough the search, the longer and more helpful would be the list of exceptions.

As his list of exceptions was compiled and the times when things were better became more identifiable, the possibility that he might be able to see the whole problem situation differently would become an option. The original labels and descriptions of the problem would no longer make sense. If they were true, then how could the exceptions take place? Was it possible that his problem might be perceived differently once his list of exceptions was developed? He would need to try it and see.

"By identifying exceptions," Michael thoughtfully uttered, "a wealth of valuable information is accumulated that provides the direction for potential solutions. Without identifiable exceptions, I would have to start from scratch in developing solutions much like 'creating a wheel.' Finding existing exceptions was like finding an existing wheel that just needed to be cleaned up in order for it to start rolling toward developing solutions once again. That would be much better."

CHAPTER 4

VERIFY THE PLAN

Michael had been really trying to change. He had benefited greatly from his time spent with Specs, the guru, and Mandrake. He had taken their wisdom, their statements, and had begun to weave them into becoming personally different. Michael truly believed in the new perspectives that his mentors had helped him discover. He was seeing his world and his relationships in it much differently. Maybe his problems were not all because of other people in his life. Michael was now able to begin to see his part in creating the difficulties he was now living out.

From his new life vantage point, his perspective was really different. He could see himself as part of his life's problems and issues. Michael had never put himself into this picture. It had always consisted of the other people who were making his life so difficult. He now saw himself as being a key player in his own relationships. If he was unable to previously see the "others" changing in order to resolve his problems, he could now see how he needed to change in order to attain the life results he was after. Wow! How different things were beginning to look. He was definitely in the process of change. He was on the move.

If he was recognizing all that was beginning to happen, how come nothing much had changed? His relationships at work remained about the same even though from time to time he had made some effort to improve them. He had checked in with Ima a few times to ask if he could do anything more to help. In a couple of meetings, he had personally initiated more participation and had asked if he could get anyone coffee when he was refilling his cup. Kim still remained distant even though he brought her flowers once and let her choose the movie on another occasion.

Michael could identify his own new efforts but was wondering if anyone else was aware of them. He now understood how hard it was to change people's opinions of him once he had been labeled in negative terms. He felt that his efforts might be too random, too infrequent, and too unorganized to create a difference that made a difference. Michael felt that all was not lost; he was definitely trying but in too much of a haphazard way. There was not enough substance or consistency in his new efforts to impact those around him that there had been significant change. It seemed like he was throwing darts at the board but that he was blindfolded. How in the world could he ever hit the bull's-eye like this? He needed to remove the blindfold. He needed more direction. He knew he was personally becoming different in a better way. The word, however, had not gotten out on the street yet. It would, he thought in a much more confident way. He would need to keep working at it. He needed to build a better mousetrap.

"Mousetrap? Mousetrap?" Michael exclaimed. "Did I say mousetrap? Yes, I did, of course I did. That was it. Now where did I see that article? Ah yes, in yesterday's newspaper in the living section," Michael said excitedly answering his own question. He rummaged through the different sections of yesterday's paper still lying on his bathroom floor. Right where he did his best reading. "There it is, right under the sports section," Michael blurted out. The article on the first page of the living section read, "How to Build a Better Relationship Mousetrap." It was written by Dr. Yuneeda Structure, a local therapist known for his work in building positive relationships.

Michael could hardly believe it. Just what the doctor ordered. He began to intently read the article when he remembered Dr. Structure was a local therapist. He asked himself, "Why am I reading this when I could be hearing it straight from the mouse's mouth?" He scanned down the article and got the doctor's phone number. He excitedly dialed the number and spoke with Minnie, Dr. Structure's office manager. She informed Michael that the first open appointment would be in six weeks. Michael's heart sank. Just as he began to feel as though the *Titanic* was sinking in the middle of his chest, Minnie asked him if he could hold on for a moment while she answered the other line. Two minutes later, Minnie was back on the line saying something about Michael having a rabbit's foot under his pillow. Before Michael could mumble out a question about rabbit's feet, Minnie was asking him if he could make tomorrow's last appointment at 5:00. Dr. Structure's client had just cancelled.

Rabbit's foot, Michael thought to himself, this was better than that. He knew all those breakfast bowls of

Lucky Charms would pay off someday. Payday was coming tomorrow as he blurted out, "Sure I'll be there, and thanks so much."

Michael set out early to Dr. Structure's office. He was taking no chances. He had decided to work through his lunch so he could leave at 4:00, giving him plenty of time. He knew that Ima needed the Starr project report by noon and the initial proposal for the Excel Inc. by 3:00. He was determined to stay on target and hit these goals making sure he did not allow himself to get distracted. The day went just as Michael had envisioned and at 4:00 on the button, he was walking out the door on his way to the office of Dr. Yuneeda Structure.

Michael was now comfortably seated in Dr. Structure's waiting room with completed forms sitting on his lap and sipping a cup of coffee provided by Minnie. He heard the doctor's door open and out came Dr. Structure walking behind his client. After saying goodbye to her, he turned to Michael and introduced himself.

"I'm Dr. Structure," he said smilingly. "Can I offer you a piece of cheese? Just kidding. With all that mousetrap talk, I think I should provide cheese and crackers in the waiting room. Come in, come in, let's talk." Michael grinningly followed Dr. Structure into his office.

After exchanging mutual pleasantries, Dr. Structure asked Michael to bring him up to date as to what his issues seemed to be and what he was doing if anything to improve them. Michael did just that. He introduced Dr. Structure to his relationships with Specs, the guru, and Mandrake. He also told Dr. Structure that although he was ready for life to get better and had somewhat randomly been working on making it happen, he was still not reaching his goal.

Planning to Plan

The first thing Dr. Structure said was, "Michael, I am very impressed with your work on your issues to date. I feel you are definitely on the right track." He then said, "You have now recognized that the problem you want to resolve in fact can be solved. How do you now use this awareness in proceeding forward? The time has come to develop a plan. This is not going to be a plan put together on a hope and a prayer. Rather, it is going to be constructed based on the new awareness about yourself that you have just discovered. You are now going to use this awareness, your identified past strengths and successes, in developing your plan."

Dr. Structure continued, "It is important to take a moment and remember that it was just a very short time ago that you were stuck and overwhelmed by your problem. Now, here you are getting ready to develop an actual plan to resolve it. That is progress and you need to recognize it! You are definitely on the solution path, but there is still work to do. Getting to this point is a real accomplishment and should energize you in moving forward with your plan development."

Michael was listening very intently. Dr. Structure then said, "You now know what the solution looks like and by identifying exceptions you know that the solution can happen. You are not at the mercy of the problem and things are not hopeless. You have identifiable strengths and successes that are available to you. It is now time to use them in formulating a plan."

Dr. Structure went on to say, "In order to reconnect with your abilities, it would be worthwhile at this time to reaffirm and reinforce what you have recently discovered.

Reviewing at this time will make it more real. Thinking and talking about your successes, making them a stronger part of your belief system will help you feel the empowerment that is now yours. You will be able to use these strengths and successes in your planning because you recognize that you really do own these abilities."

All of Michael's mentors had urged him not to forget that his productive strengths, skills, and techniques could be found in various contexts. Successes that were accomplished at home could be transferred to the workplace. Relationship successes that he had in the workplace and with friends were transferable to home and family relationships as well. Michael's ability to be successful was not limited to one context and environment. Successes could be transferred. This concept would enable him to greatly broaden his existing base of success.

"Remember, Michael," Dr. Structure went on to say, "that having problems does not doom you to having problems forever. Rather than becoming fixated on the problem, you need to understand the value of allowing yourself the opportunity to remember how you have previously resolved problems. Your search for solutions needs to incorporate the positive side of previous problem times, the side that identifies how you have resolved those previous issues. If you are unhappy in the workplace, how have you worked out problems and difficulties before? If your problem has been dealing with depression, how have you moved beyond it before? If you are having workplace difficulties, what was happening when your co-workers were more cooperative and respectful? As you now know, the answers are there and you are about ready to incorporate them in your plan."

"I understand how the feeling and personal recognition of being empowered is an important part of my planning process," Michael acknowledged. "In identifying my strengths and successes, I have become aware of the importance of the choices I make. Through these choices, I have actually had control over my past experiences. These experiences have been either successful or not based on the choices I have made. Choices can be difficult to make and have resulting consequences both positive and negative, but now I know that I control the choices I make. This is empowerment. My past strengths and successes are traceable back to the positive and constructive choices I have made. It is now time to make greater use of them in developing my plan."

Beyond Awareness

"Good news, Michael, good news," Dr. Structure emphatically shouted. "You have already begun your planning. You have gone through an analyzing process and have identified what it is you are going to plan to accomplish. This has accounted for a great deal of work, and now it is going to be put to good use. Now you are ready to go beyond the awareness of the problem, you are now ready to develop a plan to solve your problems. Just as the statement of the problem needs to be specific, the same is true for your plan. The specifics of the plan are stated in the form of the objectives and goals you wish to achieve. Loosely knit objectives present the same problems and difficulties as vaguely stated problems. They are just too difficult to work with, will drain your energies, and have you running all over the place accomplishing something other than attaining your real goals and objectives. You look busy and you are, you just are not getting done what needs to get done."

After Beyond Awareness
Options . . . Brainstorming II

"I certainly have been there before," Michael acknowledged. "I am beginning to identify and realize that in order to develop more than one way to solve a problem, plan options need to be generated. Brainstorming to develop multiple plan options need to take place. If there was only one way to communicate effectively, work efficiently, be a good friend, find fun and enjoyment in life, develop a loving, caring relationship, etc. I would certainly be in *big* trouble. Fortunately for me, life does not work that way. There are many ways to achieve my goals, and no way is the right way. They all represent different ways to reach my objectives. This is why brainstorming to create multiple options is so important and necessary in developing successful plans. I am ready to work on developing plans."

Reaching Our Goals . . . Pipe
Dream or Reality

"Since you have previously identified the goals you want to attain, you are ready to establish and develop sound priorities and specific objectives," Dr. Structure began. "It is these specific objectives, developed from brainstorming options that will clearly identify your plan. They will also help you manage your time better since your energies and efforts will be directed toward accomplishing your stated objectives. You have a target to hit. Anything off target will be identified as such, which will allow you to stay focused and able to concentrate on making your identified goal a reality.

"In order for you to reach the goals you set, you need to develop plans to pave the way. The difference between pipe dreams and reality, Michael, is that you plan for reality. Pipe dreams are just supposed to happen. Developing a plan for a pipe dream is a necessity in order for it to become a reality."

$4 \times W + H = Plan$

Dr. Structure had instructed Michael to remember that establishing objectives identified what it was he wanted to accomplish. This was a good place to start when developing his plan. Dr. Structure added, "In order to make your plan work, however, the integral parts of your plan need to be identified. The formula that makes planning work requires establishing the who, what, where, when, and how of the plan. Once these facets are identified, the plan will take on its specific substance and identity.

"Let's take a look at your workplace issue more specifically as Specs would say Michael." Dr. Structure continued, "if your plan is to get more cooperation and involvement from your workplace team in helping do necessary project responsibilities, then the following questions need to be answered in order for the objectives to be reached. *Who* is going to do the necessary tasks? This could be done in a variety of ways, but it does need to be specifically identified. Will each team member choose one responsibility until all the responsibilities are distributed? Will team members be assigned their specific responsibilities? Will they be able to trade or choose different responsibilities at a later time?"

"*What* are the project responsibilities that need to be done? They need to be listed so that everyone involved will have this information. *Where* do the people involved need to be to accomplish the goals? In your situation, you are identifying the workplace as the location where the tasks need to take place."

"*When* do the tasks need to be completed? It is important to remember that time lines and limits are critical in planning. When do the goals and objectives need to be met? By next week, the end of the quarter, or by June 1? Without time limits, the identification of when 'it' needs to happen will be very difficult to determine and could allow 'it' to continue indefinitely. Establishing the 'when' moves the process along to an identifiable conclusion. Without it, the objective will always get done later, or will be an ongoing process never quite reaching conclusion.

"*How* will the plan be accomplished? *How* will you know if the plan is working? *How* will you evaluate it? Will you make a chart that tracks the plan, and will there be a reward for successful accomplishment? Will there be less arguing? Will you be less stressed and fatigued? These are all good questions Michael that need good answers.

"There is no right plan other than the plan you create for yourself. As long as you ask yourself the 4×W+H questions and answer them specifically, you will have developed a workable plan, a structured plan. Although you want to start with the best plan you can initially create, you also want to keep in mind that you can always revise or modify your plan later if necessary."

SMAC Me Please

"Fortunately for me, Dr. Structure," Michael responded, "I like to plan, and I seem to be good at it. Today is a pretty good example of my creating a plan and successfully carrying it out in scheduling my work so I could make my appointment on time."

"Quite impressive," Dr. Structure had told Michael. "In order to help develop your best possible plan, you will need to take a look at what you are really trying to accomplish. What are the objectives you want to attain? Without properly defining your goals, you will not reach them. Instead, you will wind up reaching something else other than what you want, still being left with the unresolved problem. Getting here today on time took good planning on your part."

Dr. Structure then gave Michael the criteria for setting meaningful objectives. "I'm going to talk some smack to you, Michael, that I want you to remember. This is objective setting smack, and it is important to know and understand it if your objectives are going to be met. All your objectives need to meet these four SMAC criteria. In order to successfully fulfill objective setting structure they must be:

"*Specific*, so that they are described in detailed and precise enough terms to provide the expected end result and eliminate potential misunderstanding.

"*Measureable*, which makes it possible to quantify the change from where you start in comparison to where you wind up. Here are a couple of examples," Dr. Structure offered. "Going from taking no time for personal activities per week to spending four hours per week on yourself.

Going from completing three work projects per week to completing five projects per week.

"*Attainable*, which considers that we never know what we can attain until we 'go for it,' but recognizes that objectives do need to be realistically set in order to be accomplished.

"*Compatible*, that allows for our objectives to 'fit' with our lifestyle and other objectives we have set forth for ourselves. Specifically, if we want to stay employed by our present employer, our objective in developing better communication with our boss needs to take this into consideration."

Dr. Structure leaned forward as he said, "These objective-setting criteria will keep you on track to attain what needs to happen in order to modify or eliminate your problems. For whatever reasons, many times you may not include all four of the objective criteria. Usually you get an idea of what needs to be done, set an objective, and just go for it. You should be congratulated for your enthusiasm and initiative but without objective setting criteria and structure that are adhered to, you will somehow miss your target, allowing the problem to further mushroom."

S—"That is why we need to revisit our SMAC structure once more," the good doctor stated. "Since there is a need to think about whether your objective is specific enough, developed objectives will need to be challenged. Is it really going to accomplish what you are intending to accomplish? Will others know what you want them to be doing so there is no confusion that leads to excuses or failure? As previously discussed, can the following 4×W+H questions be answered?" Dr. Structure asked.

"Let me give it a shot, Doc," Michael volunteered.

"Who is involved? What is the specific result that will be achieved? Where will the work on the objective be done? When will accomplishing the objective begin, and when do we expect it to end? How will we reach our goal and track and evaluate the progress we are making? The answers to these questions will result in the development of more specifically set objectives," Michael said proudly.

M—"Michael, that was great," Dr. Structure said admiringly. "Remember, however, that just setting an objective may seem enough by itself, but it is not. Wanting relationships to improve, getting team members to help more, or feeling less anxious at work are certainly good things to have happen. They do not, however, answer the question of how you will be able to identify the needed change in measurable rather than general terms. It is truly a question of identifying accountability. Being able to identify what needs to be done and who needs to do it will allow you to be able to measure and evaluate your objectives in other than a subjective way."

A—"Let's also take a closer look at ensuring that our goals are attainable," Dr. S. stated invitingly. "Since you are the one setting your objectives, you must feel that you can in fact achieve them. The objectives do need to be attainable." Michael smilingly added, "I know I would like to make a million dollars this year or never argue with Kim again, but would these objectives be realistic and attainable? I would need to answer this question when setting my personal objectives."

"You are absolutely correct," Dr. Structure agreed. "Continuing to attempt to achieve objectives out of our reach is self-defeating, is a waste of effort, and will drain your available energy that eventually will eliminate change from actually occurring in your life. In order to be productive, it is necessary to make your objectives attainable objectives."

C—"Lastly, Michael, don't forget that in order to reach the objectives you set, they need to fit with other objectives and priorities in your life. An objective cannot be contradictory to other objectives you have set for yourself. Compatibility means that the accomplishment of one objective does not conflict with your other overall life goals."

Dr. Structure now leaned back somewhat. His points had been made. He went on to say, "Therefore, Michael, when setting objectives it is necessary to allow enough time to give thought to these criteria, to this structure. This means that there is a need to commit enough time to evaluate whether your objectives are specific, measurable, attainable, and compatible. If the time and thought is committed to up front, the end result will be the achievement of an objective that is truly meaningful. If the goal is meaningful, then the plan developed to reach it also needs to be meaningful and worth the time, effort, and energy it takes to develop it."

You're the One

"Oh, and one last thing, Michael," Dr. Structure added, "in developing your plan, you need to remember that you will not be able to rely on the participation or cooperation of others. Therefore, do not plan their expected or desired behavior into your plan. You will need to remember that the only person's behavior you will be able to control is yours. A plan in which change is built around other people changing is leading you toward potential disappointment.

"There is a very positive point to be made for you maintaining responsibility and accountability in working toward developing change you want to attain. The most optimistic feature about the change process is that one person can produce change. Other people in relationship with you may not be as motivated to work on the relationship and your objectives as you are. However, if just one person, *you*, makes the initial change, the others will find themselves needing to change in response. They will discover that you do not tolerate their usual and normal behavior in the same way. Therefore as you no longer remain the same, it becomes necessary for them in some way to now respond differently. This is the process of change. This is how change occurs. Michael, you be Da Man!"

Michael continued to hear Dr. Structure's words long after they had been uttered. This was the structure that he had been seeking. The necessity and importance of having a plan to move from where he was to where he wanted to be. There was no doubt in his mind that he was going to be responsible for developing the needed plan to reach the objectives that he had set out to attain in his life. No one else could do what he needed to do for himself.

Both Dr. Structure and Michael stood up. They reached out and shook each other's hand and then gave one another a meaningful, sincere hug. "I feel that there has been a connection between us, Dr. Structure," Michael said emotionally. "This has been very important to me. This has been tremendously helpful. This has provided an additional piece that I knew had been missing. You have given me so much meaningful information." Michael had plenty to think about as he left the office of Dr. Yuneeda Structure.

At the End of the Day

Through this process of change, Michael had now become ready to go beyond the awareness of his problem and was now ready to develop a plan to solve his problem. By developing brainstorming options, plans with sound priorities and specific objectives would begin to be identified. Moving these plans into reality rather than having them remain pipe dreams is what needed to come next.

In developing his specific plan, he would need to use the 4×W+H=PLAN formula. The who, what, where, when, and how of his plan would then become established. This is where he would actually start putting his plan together. As long as he asked himself the 4×W+H questions and answered them specifically, he would have developed a workable plan. Although he wanted to start with the best plan he could initially create, he would keep in mind that he could always revise or modify his plan later if necessary.

He would need to properly define meaningful objectives in order to reach the goals he planned to attain. His objectives then needed to meet the four SMAC criteria and structure. They needed to be specific, measurable, attainable, and compatible. This was the time to take the time to go through each of the SMAC criteria, as all four of them would need to be met if his objectives were going to be attained. If the needed time and thought was committed to the plan in the beginning, the end result would be the achievement of an objective that was truly meaningful.

In the development of his plan, it was important to remember that this was his plan. Since it was his, he would need to keep in mind that he could not rely on the participation or cooperation of others to make it successful. It might be that people around him would be supportive and helpful and then again, they may not. In any case, it was important to remember that he was The One. This was what change was all about. His ability to solve his own problems.

Now that Michael was back home and had taken time to digest his visit with Dr. Structure, he felt that the time to put his personal plan together had arrived and not a moment too soon. Rumors were flying again at work that at the end of the year, three months from now, Ajax would be making their "final" employee cutbacks.

"Oh, oh," Michael involuntarily said, "I need to start being the new me *now*! I will have enough time to create my new reputation, but there is not a minute to lose. I will not be any better prepared to create my plan than I am right now," Michael uttered in the privacy of his home. "It is time to put this all together. It is time to move forward," he said in a committed tone of voice.

Michael began thinking to himself, *Let's see, my workplace issues. I think I'll start with those. Specifically, I need to complete my work on time without getting diverted by other things that seemingly always are coming up. In fact, more specifically, I need to stay focused on my prioritized work assignments until they are completed. I bet when I accomplish this, my coworkers will find me more appealing to work with. I am sure Ima Watchingu will. I am really a very nice guy once people get to know me. Not getting my part of the project completed on time is like having a boulder between me and my* team members. They can never get close enough to like me. Hmmmm. I think I need to give them more of an opportunity to do so.

So, my specific goal is to stay focused on my prioritized work assignments until they are completed. Good, there is my goal. Now for creating the plan that will make it happen. Let me get that formula that Dr. Structure gave me going: $4 \times W + H = PLAN$. I need to fill in the who, what, where, when, and how blanks. Well the "who" is pretty simple. I am the "who." I need to make sure that I have my work prioritized correctly. I also need to make sure I am staying on task in getting it done no matter what else comes up. Let's see if there are any other people that I need besides myself. Ima Watchingu, she is part of the "who." She needs to assign me the work she needs from me so that I have enough time to get it done. Then there are my teammates. They are also part of the "who." I need to keep them up to date on my progress. Meeting along the way with Pam, Larry, Andrew, and Nancy (the PLAN team) for lunch or coffee might help in keeping them updated and more comfortable with the project's progress. There, I think those are all of the "who."

Now let me give some thought to the "what" needs to be done. I already know that I need to be more organized and prioritized. Really it is not particularly surprising to me that I miss deadlines and even meetings because everything is so scattered. Scattered like me. So what I need to do every morning when I get to work is to make a "to-do" list. On it, I need to list all of the things I need to do that day at work. Then once my list is made, I need to set priorities as to which items are most important. The most important gets a 1 by it, the next most important gets a 2, and so on. Wow, this would certainly give me a whole new awareness for the day. As new things come up during the day, I will be able to stay focused on the most important work to complete. Right now it seems that I am just stumbling into work assignments as I discover them on my desk. This "what" I need to do is quite different from the reality I am living.

Thank goodness the "where" is easy. For the most part, the "where" is at my workplace, Ajax. Sometimes the "where" might shift to my apartment if I need to continue to work on it after hours.

The "when" really gives me something to think about. It is not just doing the work, it is doing it in the timeframe it needs to be completed. That is definitely part of my problem. I might complete the assigned work but wind up finishing it late, which throws a lot of people off schedule. This is when I usually see "that look" on Pam's, Larry's, Andrew's, and Nancy's faces. It is saying, "You are really a pain in the butt, and a difficult person to like." I will be very happy not to see that look ever again. I think what I will do is to put a place for the due date on my prioritized list, so I do not lose track of my time responsibilities. Speaking of track, that is what I need to do. I need to track where I am on the project relative to when it is due to see if I need to modify my plan. That should really help keep me on schedule.

Last but certainly not least is the "how" I am going to get all of this done. I have built a lot of my "how" into my who, what, where, and when description. I do know the "how" I am going to do this needs to be actually applied. Knowing all of these planning elements without their application will be an effort in futility.

Now all I need to do is to incorporate some SMAC into my plan to make sure it meets the requirements of good planning. I need to revisit my goal as well as my entire plan to *make sure it is specific. It would seem that I have done a good job on this. Specs would be proud of me. No vague, generic concepts in my plan. Instead I have used specific language to attain specific results. Good work if I do say so myself.*

I need to make sure there are identified timeframes, so I can measure how I am doing throughout the planned process. In doing this, I am ensuring that if I get behind in my work, I will at least have a definite awareness of that taking place. In this way, I will have time to do something about it. I can modify my plan if necessary to make sure I meet my deadlines and goals. That will be a huge improvement.

My goals and plan to reach them seem pretty realistic to me. I need to be honest with myself in making sure I am maximizing my efforts but also realistic enough not to provide myself with a continual overload that I will not be able to achieve. I think I have identified an attainable balance.

All of this goal setting and planning is definitely compatible with my overall professional and life goals. I want to be successful. I want to have a future at Ajax and all of this will help me achieve it.

"Unbelievable," Michael could not help himself from shouting. "I have done it. It did take some time, effort, and energy but doesn't everything that is worth doing? What a difference in how I have typically gone about doing things," he continued elatedly. "I feel so much better, so much calmer, and in control. I can hardly wait to get to work to put all of this in motion. I feel totally confident that with this plan, I won't have to worry about layoffs at Ajax. In fact with this plan, I think I will check out Ajax's retirement benefits."

Speaking of retirement, Michael continued thinking, *I definitely know who I want to retire with . . . Kim of course.*

That will never happen, however, unless I start planning for it now. I know Kim is getting weary of our relationship. She is not getting enough of what she wants from me. She has told me about my lack of expressed affection and that she definitely does not feel like she is #1 in my life. She said that she feels like a very distant Avis.

The changes I have begun to make have not been consistent enough to create the change she is looking for, and I want to give her. I think at the most, I have the same three months with Kim as I do with Ajax. I have even noticed her looking at our waiters in a different way lately. Not a good sign. Not good at all. I need to work at least as hard if not harder on Kim's plan, or I will be in the unemployed boyfriend line in a heartbeat.

When I was able to observe my problems resolved with Kim, I became aware of specifically what I need to do. In order to be more affectionate to Kim, I have to express my caring and love for her on a consistent basis by doing things for her and with her. There, a specific goal waiting for a specific plan, rather than my typical random plan. Thank goodness I know how to do this. I need to get started.

Thanks to Dr. Structure, I know exactly where to begin when creating my plan: $4 \times W + H = PLAN$. Thanks, Doc, Michael thought sincerely. *Definitely in any plan with Kim I am needing to be the "who." I need to start doing things that will make my plan successful. Kim could be part of the "who" as well by giving me feedback as to how my plan is working. However, I know I am going to be relying only on myself.*

"What" I need to do is stated in my plan. I need to express my caring and love for Kim on a consistent basis. This would entail my doing things for her and with her. Let's see, that would include bringing her weekly "surprises" like flowers or

note cards or the Jerry Garcia ice cream she loves so much. I could also schedule weekly time for us to be together rather than the hit or miss way I see Kim right now. We could also take turns planning our "fun times" together so that it is not so much about me. It can be about us. I could also help out by taking over specific household stuff when I stay over at her place. She would definitely love it if I clean up after we eat. How about helping her set up and clean up when we have our friends come over? Boy, would she be pleasantly surprised! After all, I don't want to be a guest. I want to be a partner. Those are some pretty good starters for the "what" that needs to be part of my plan.

The "where" includes many locations. "Where" I need to put my plan into operation includes Kim's apartment and mine, restaurants that we go to, concerts that we rock out at, movies that we see as well as other places that come up "where" I can express my love and caring for her. I need to keep my antennae up for opportunities where I can use my plan.

"When" is simple to figure out. Yesterday was one day too late to get started. Three months and the clock is ticking. That creates enough "when" motivation for me. I don't want that ticking to be a time bomb that is going to blow our relationship apart. I want it to be counting down to a celebration of our everlasting love. It is up to me to choose which it will be. I also need to stay aware of specific opportunities that will give me a chance to express my love spontaneously "when" these situations arise.

"How" will all of this happen? By my committed dedication to making it happen. The sum of all of these plan parts create the "how." I need to make the math work by doing what I have planned to do. That will be "how" the plan will become successful.

Now I just need to SMAC my plan so I am sure it is airtight. Let's see, it is definitely specific. The t's have been crossed and the i's dotted. The measurement will be identified by the increased number of caring, loving actions I express. I am planning to make what Kim can now count on one hand to having her needing to buy an abacus to keep track of them all.

My plan is absolutely attainable. I have included only those things that I can do and am willing to do. I cannot wait to start showing Kim as well as myself that I am now ready to "walk my talk." Without question, my plan is compatible with what I want to happen and be part of my life. My plan creates the life I want to be living with the woman I want to be living it with.

"Now that is what I call a plan," Michael shouted triumphantly.

5

EXECUTE . . . JUST DO IT!

A huge void had been filled. Michael now had formulated his plan; he had his direction. Things no longer felt disorganized or haphazard. He knew what he needed to do and had equated his 4×W+H formula. For the first time in a very long time, Michael felt in control; he felt empowered to now do what he had been capable of doing for some time. He had put it together, he was ready to go.

Michael felt energized. What a perfect time to have a session with his personal trainer Buzz Nike. He liked Buzz a lot. He was so positive, a real action person. When Michael walked into the gym, he saw Buzz in the middle of the exercise area doing his own personal work out. That's Buzz. Not a man who just talks the talk. Buzz was always ready to walk the walk. Well in Buzz's case, run the run. Michael caught Buzz's eye, and he jogged over with his hand already extended. He vigorously shook Michael's hand and provided a few sincere welcoming back slaps in his greeting.

"Wow," Buzz said, "you look great. You look like weights have literally been lifted off your shoulders. What happened, man, how are things going?" Michael felt even better. So it showed did it, great. Nothing like a positive glow to shed a new light on life.

"Do you have a few minutes between workouts?" Michael asked. "Here, let me buy the first round of carrot juice. You know you can't resist that offer, Buzz." Michael led Buzz over to the juice bar. He began to tell Buzz all about his current journey. Buzz was impressed and expressed his enthusiasm to Michael.

"I can't tell you how happy I am for you, Michael," Buzz said. "I've always felt a real bond with you and could feel the strain you have been under. I consider myself not only your personal trainer but also your personal friend. That's why I want to give you a heads-up. I can't tell you how many people I see with great expectations of becoming fit and getting into shape. It's not that they are not sincere in what they want to accomplish, they just fall short of doing it. They don't pull the trigger. Michael, there is a reason I only carry Nike equipment at my gym. Sure, they make great products, but boy, their slogan, 'Just Do It,' says it all."

Long Live Nike

"What a great solutions statement that is," Buzz continued. "You can talk forever about what needs to be done, what you used to do, and all the reasons why what you want to do either can or cannot be done. However, at some moment in time, your plan needs to be executed, you need to 'Just Do It'!"

"Wow, Buzz, that sounds so scary," Michael said in a concerned tone.

"You better believe it," Buzz responded. "Everything that I have been doing preparing for this moment is on the line," Michael stated thoughtfully. "It now is all sounding so much like real life. I guess that's because it is. Whether it is taking the training wheels off my first bike or deciding to become successful at Ajax Advertising, today is going to be the actual day that change happens. It is time to come out of the bleachers, to come off the sideline and onto the playing field. I can now see that I am playing the game of life, and I am now a player and not a spectator."

"Up to this point, my awareness of my problems and how to deal with them has been increased, as identified in my meetings with Specs, the guru, and Mandrake. Then in my meeting with Dr. Structure, I was able to develop a plan to move my newfound awareness forward into the planning stage. Now, the next step involves applying the plan and most importantly 'Doing It.' This is the most critical step of all. Is everything that I have done so far going to be meaningful or just an exercise?"

Don't Analyze to Paralyze
You Have Prepared for This Moment

"Michael," Buzz interjected, "There might be many reasons why taking this action step will be difficult for you. Even though the situation you are experiencing and the effect it is having on your life is not what you want, it is what you know. It is this trade-off of the known for the unknown that can make you hesitate. 'Doing' is the first step into 'newness.' Taking action is a brave act because you are not positively sure as to the result of your bravery."

"Wait a minute," Michael thought out loud to himself. "I have not reached this point, executing the plan, 'Doing It,' by accident." He began to revisit his recent journey. He had worked hard in developing a statement of the specific problem. He knew what he was wanting resolved. He had focused on and had identified what his problems were that needed to be solved. He had then observed the problem resolved. He had already been there in his mind's eye. He had visited the unknown and knew what it needed to look like in order for there to be a solution to his problems. He had identified exceptions to his problem, when the problem had been managed successfully. He was no longer creating the solution wheel, instead he was trying to find where he had last left it, and he had remembered. Using these past strengths and successes, he had developed a plan, one that was built on a solid base and foundation. He had set objectives, which met the criteria of being specific, measurable, attainable, and compatible. Now he was ready to put his plan into action.

"You know, Buzz," Michael said convincingly, "now that I have given the unknown some thought, I am ready to meet it head-on. None of what I am preparing to do is haphazard at all. I am following specific steps to solve my problems, and my plan is well conceived and thought through. I really believe that I would paralyze myself from inaction if I did not move forward at this time. This is why 'Doing It' should not pose the same concern and fears as before I started the process. I am ready and prepared for this moment. This is a new feeling for dealing with my problems, to actually be prepared to move forward. This position, however, did not just materialize out of nowhere. I have worked hard to get here, and this is my reward. I am now able to make it happen, to *just do it*!"

Making Known the Unknown
Who's Afraid of the Boogeyman

Michael definitely felt stronger in challenging the unknown. The unknown should have its limits of concern. In a step-by-step fashion, he had challenged the unknown. The unknown was now his ally not an enemy as it may have been in the past. This was different. He was changing, and he had empowered himself to continue to move forward. All of his preparation was about to pay off.

"Buzz, I know what the unknown looks like. I have observed it, I have planned for it, and I am prepared for it," Michael said confidently. "The unknown, what I am moving toward, is change. It is the beginning of difference in my life. It is what needs to come next. It is what will get me off the spot I have been stuck on. The change process has allowed me to get to this new place of hope. By 'Doing It,' by working and applying my plan, the unknown is about to become known. I am on my way!

Bursting Through the Barricades

"You know something, Michael," Buzz responded. "I can now see you winning the race, resolving your old problems. If making change take place has previously been difficult, taking the "Just Do It" step will provide a new, different, and exciting experience. This is what 'doing' is all about, getting beyond where you normally stop. It is moving forward through barriers that previously ended your journey. Those barricades need to be removed," Buzz emphatically stated pounding his clenched fist on the juice bar.

"Many times our past describes how we are in the present," Buzz said thoughtfully. "If for the most part, you have not made decisions for yourself, doing so now may seem like a strange and difficult task. As we go through the process of growing up and becoming our own person, 'others' may impose their desires and realities on us. We learn to do and become what others tell us rather than realizing we have the ability and right to make our own choices. If for many years of our life we are told and taught to live by choices others impose on us then that becomes our reality. Others then make our choices and our job is to please them or obey them, even though as time goes on, this may become more difficult to do. Your problems therefore, may not have appeared to be resolvable since your experience in resolving them had been limited. This, however, is no longer the case. It is time for change!"

"Michael, I see it all the time in the work I do with my clients, with the work I have done with you," Buzz continued. "Your past inability to 'Do It' may have been based in the dilemma of 'Do What?' When we are in the throes of a problem that is overwhelming we may get overcome by a feeling of hopelessness. It is this hopelessness that paralyzes and disables us from thinking about a way out. There is no way out, there is no light at the end of the tunnel, no glimmer of hope. Hopelessness, however, is diminished or eliminated through the process of change."

Michael totally agreed. The "Do What" dilemma, not being able to identify solution options, had also been derailed by his newly developed brainstorming process. This option development process allowed him to be able to develop that glimmer of hope that was so identifiably absent in his life. He now had it. In fact, he now owned the tools to work through what previously had been debilitating problems.

"To tell you the truth, Buzz," Michael confessed, "Up until very recently it was certainly a probability that my problems would have remained problems if all I had as solution firepower were my same blanks or no ammunition at all. Up to this point, it had not been a fair fight, but now it is different. Through my journey to create change, I have become prepared not only to fight through my problems but also to win the battle. It is this quality of being prepared that is now making a difference in my ability to move on. As has been pointed out on many occasions, the change process provides me with the ability to deal with my issues in a prepared, organized manner. This message needs to be continually repeated in the hope that repetition will help reinforce in my mind and belief system that I really am prepared and therefore ready to *just do it*!"

Does Anyone Have the Time?

"Michael, from what I am hearing and seeing," Buzz interjected, "it seems that the time is now right for you to work on resolving the problems you face. That is a major problem in itself you know, taking the time. If you are like most people, there just does not seem to be enough time in the day to get things done."

"I could not agree with your more," Michael concurred. "I always seem to be busy with work, household responsibilities that seem endless, keeping up relationships (friends, family, Kim), taking care of 'things,' calling people back three times before anything gets done, plus handling the endless list of miscellaneous stuff that just happens. It seems I am stuck with my problems because there never seems like there is enough time to resolve them.

"Whether my time management skills are subpar or my priorities are confused, the bottom line is I just do not take the time I need in order to move forward," Michael continued.

"Everything worthwhile takes some amount of time to accomplish," Buzz added. "Solutions are no different. Prioritizing your time to work out your problems will pay big dividends not only for yourself but also for those people around you as well."

Risky Business

"I know you have been receiving a lot of advice lately," Buzz acknowledged. Michael thought about all the recent advice he had received. "It is always easy for others to give advice," Buzz continued. "Their risk in you carrying out your plan is limited. Yours is greater. Risk taking can be a deterrent to doing. If you are like most people, you do not like taking risks. In fact, you might avoid taking risks like the plague. You might be afraid of what might happen if you behave in a way that is outside of your normal pattern. Even when your normal existing behavior does not make you happy or is itself the problem, the thought of risking doing something different such as attempting a new solution might be out of your comfort zone and realm of possibility. Again, this will keep you stuck in the muck and mire of the problem of inaction."

"I used to be that person," Michael admitted, "but now it is different. Having a process that I can trust and believe in helps reduce the risk of change. My new process is built on sound principles . . . Mine! I specifically describe the problem. I observe the problem-resolved future. I find previous life experience exceptions when the problem was manageable. I develop my own plan based on my identified strengths and successes. Now I am ready to *just do it* to execute my plan. Yes, there are risks, but I have incorporated them in establishing my planned objectives and in my plan development. Because I have developed a sound plan and have worked through the steps of the change process, I am ready to take the anticipated associated risks of my actions. I have reached the point of being aware that there are as many if not more risks in not "Doing It" than in actually putting my plan into action. The time is now!"

Perfection Is Too Perfect

"One word of caution," Buzz warned. "Try not to be a perfectionist. You need to understand plans are evolutionary. What you start with today is not necessarily what you will continue with down the road. The idea of having to have the 'perfect' plan in order to 'Do It' will delay the plan application indefinitely and unnecessarily."

Perfect was a scary word. It was something, a place he could never reach. Michael had carried with him various messages that he had received from others throughout his life. He had experienced the "need to be perfect in order to be accepted" type messages throughout his life, which made the "Doing It" stage more difficult to initiate.

If he did not need his plan to be perfect in order to begin to implement it, then what was good enough? Conscientiously following his new process was definitely good enough.

"I certainly understand the problem of needing to be perfect Buzz," Michael admitted. "Fortunately, I have created a plan that is well thought through and developed. Implementing this plan I created will allow change to occur. It will move me off my stuck spot. Whatever imperfections my plan contains, they will not deter the impact of my moving forward in my life. I need to apply my plan with all its imperfections. I need to *just do it*!"

Taking Baby Steps

Buzz interrupted Michael's thoughts by asking, "Hey Michael, are you a movie buff?" Michael nodded affirmatively several times.

"Did you ever see *What About Bob*? One of the greatest flicks ever," said Buzz emphatically.

"A real classic," Michael replied smilingly. "Well, the part that seems to be a great fit at the moment," Buzz explained, "was when the therapist in the movie talks to his clients about the importance of taking 'baby steps' in working through their problems. Although presented in a very humorous way, the message happens to be a very good one, especially right now. Going from point A to point Z is too much to accomplish at one time. It is too risky. It is like eating an elephant. Don't try to do it in one bite. Many truly great accomplishments get overlooked because we look immediately to the end result and anything other than that is identified as being unsuccessful.

"We live in a fast-paced world that is designed to give us what we want *now*! We want the whole enchilada, the finished product, the end result not in bits and pieces, but in its entirety. So it is not surprising that we have developed this limited patience level approach to life. Look around. Do you see the flashing neon signs and the store logos stating one-hour dry cleaning, we deliver your pizza in thirty minutes or it is free, shoe repair while you wait, fast-food restaurant after fast-food restaurant etc.?

"Is it any wonder then, that in most situations our ability to appreciate the process that leads to successful conclusions is extremely limited or nonexistent? It is this process, that you are now being asked to recognize. Your movement from A to B is important and appreciating the effort, energy, and commitment that it takes to get there is necessary in order to get to Z. The expectations we have of ourselves or that others have of us, or those we think they have of us, can also make recognizing the smallest measure of success difficult. Expectations whether realistic, rational, logical, or not, do become our reality. We measure our success as to how we measure up to expectations.

"Expectations can run extremely high. We may be expected to handle our problems immediately or not have problems at all. If this is the case, then small steps may not count. Once the plan is put into application, immediate success and nothing less than that is acceptable. There are no small victories. The only victory that is recognized or that counts is the total attainment of the plan's objectives.

"The other extreme is that of low expectations or no expectation of achieving success. Throughout our life, we may have been told that we are a failure. That we are incompetent and have little or no ability to put a plan together much less make it work. How could we possibly put together a workable plan when these are the messages we carry with us? Is there any reason to identify small measures of success when we do not think it is possible to be successful?

"Obviously, neither of these extreme positions is helpful in identifying the needed successful steps necessary to reach my planned objectives," Michael stated in total agreement. "What would be helpful are expectations that fall between these two extremes. In this way, it would be allowable for the achievement of small steps to be attained and recognized in reaching my final goal."

Catch Yourself Doing Something Right
Track Success

Michael was itching to get started. He began thinking about how he would know when he had begun to solve his own issues. Since "Doing It" was not easy and could take a good bit of courage, it was important that his efforts did not go unnoticed. "Buzz, I have been thinking that it would be terrific if there were someone who was there to pat me on the back as I move forward in the execution of my plan," Michael said thoughtfully. "Maybe there will be. Maybe not. Well, I am here and I know that what I have done thus far is helping to solve my problems. I need to keep track of what I am doing right.

"Maybe keeping a journal or making a chart would help," Buzz suggested. "Many of the clients I work with do that. You need to celebrate your new victories, your movement toward your objectives. You need to reward yourself. You might buy yourself something or take yourself someplace you have wanted to go. At the very least you need to congratulate yourself on getting unstuck and moving ahead," Buzz added enthusiastically.

Doing Takes Doing

It had become crystal clear to Michael that "Just Do It" involves just that. Buzz Nike was right. The execution of developed plans does not just happen. Walking the walk is much more involved than just talking the talk. Anyone can say what they are going to do. "Doing It," however, is something else. Everything up to the point of execution is certainly necessary, but as can be seen, the doing is what gets it done. Buzz turned back to Michael after grabbing a slice of orange and said, "Okay, pal, *let's do it!*"

At the End of the Day

Upon arriving home after a great but exhausting work out, Michael once again checked his shoes. They did say Nike on them. He was now going to *just do it!* Because he had worked hard to get to this point, he had certainly arrived prepared. He was not paralyzed from inaction; he was ready to move forward. His process had made taking this action step easier since he had made known what previously had been the unknown. He knew what change looked like and what he needed to do to attain it. He had worked through old messages that had barricaded him from moving on and now understood that taking no action could be riskier than taking the action necessary to resolve his problems. It did not get any better than this; it was as "perfect" as it was going to be. It was time to *just do it*!

Speaking of time, Michael needed to make some. This was the first thing he could do, create the time he would need to get done what he needed to accomplish. He was now ready to review his plan identifying what the "baby steps" were that needed to be taken in order to go from A to B on his journey to Z. Executing his plan, "Doing It," involved just that, a lot of doing. It certainly would make him feel better as he began to move toward his goal, but this Doing part was a lot of work. There was a necessary investment of time, effort, and energy that needed to be made in order to make his process work. But you know something Michael thought, it was worth it!

Now that he had started doing, he needed to continue to do. He needed to follow his plan, one step at a time, feeling the empowerment along the way of getting closer to achieving his objectives. It was important as part of the "Just Do It" process that he caught himself doing something right. This meant that he would need to track his success. As he was now putting his plan into action, Michael needed to make sure that he took the time to evaluate how well he was doing. He needed to reward himself along the way, celebrating his success!

Michael knew that there was no greater thrill than the thrill of success of accomplishment. Knowing that he had set out to achieve a certain goal and was actually reaching it was a wonderfully empowering experience. It was the knowing that whatever the problem was that he was presently facing, he had the power and control in his life to make change happen. He could *do it*! He now owned that ability. He was now prepared and able to process himself through any and all problem situations that might arise. He was ready, prepared, and able to *just do it*!

AT THE END OF THE DAY ... AGAIN

Everyone Michael had sought out seemed to have *the answer* . . . at least for themselves. Specs was so certain that understanding the specifics of Michael's problems would lead to the answer. Just as certain as to the answer was the guru only his answer was different. Being able to observe the resolution of the problem would alleviate the issue. The guru had been so sure and confident of his answer that Michael was almost embarrassed to think that there needed to be more. Besides, the guru was a guru, and who could argue with a guru?

How could Michael forget Mandrake? With all of those portraits of the great magicians, it was difficult to challenge his mystical and magical powers. What was Mandrake's message? Oh yes. All that was needed to resolve Michael's problems was an ability to be able to focus on the exceptions. Having the ability to identify the successful times in

Michael's life would enable him to replicate them. It was all too easy to focus on the immediate failures that Michael was experiencing and forget the times when he had already been a more productive, successful person. What made those successful times different? What was he forgetting? What had he done better in dealing with past difficulties? Mandrake's advice was certainly good advice; it just didn't seem to Michael that this focus would be enough.

Then there was Dr. Structure. Wow! What credentials. An MBA in business with an MA in psychology and a PhD in organizational management. He had even taught at UCLA and USC After working at IBM. This guy made Campbell's alphabet soup look like they were missing a few letters. Plan, plan, plan. That was Dr. Structure's message. Ready, fire, aim. You would never hit the target with that process. What a great line. That planning, that aiming was certainly important in being able to hit the target. Michael was beginning to get dizzy with all of this thinking. Could everyone have the answer? Was everyone right or was everyone wrong? Michael's struggling was creating even another problem for himself, that of struggling with his struggle.

Michael had never met anyone like Buzz Nike. What a guy. What a philosophy. Execute . . . just do it! Right out of the shoe ads and boy, did they sell a lot of shoes. There had to be some truth in that "Just Do It" statement.

Michael eventually wore himself out. He fell into a deep, exhausted sleep. At the end of the day, he had all the answers he was seeking and at the same time he felt he had not found the way to put them all together. Slowly the next morning, he began to awake. Only it was not the next morning. It was 3:00 the next afternoon. All of his thinking, his trying to put it all together, had taken everything out of him. However, he was now feeling different. He couldn't quite identify it yet, but he felt stronger. As everything had been taken out of him, it seemed to allow a new set of everything to take its place. He was filled with a new awareness, a new enthusiasm, and a new strength. *He had figured it out!* Finally, it had all come together. The answer was not hidden any longer. The answer was his.

No one had the answer for Michael. It was Michael who had his own answer. His search had not been futile. In fact, it had opened Michael's awareness to what he now believed would be an approach to his problems that would lead to resolutions. It had always been there, within him waiting to be discovered.

The answer had not been provided by any one person Michael had sought out on his journey. Life was not quite that simple. It had dawned on Michael while he had been asleep and as his mind cleared from all the information and answers he had accumulated, that everyone had been right in their own way. It was not any one answer that had been provided to Michael; it had been the totality of all the answers. Most importantly, Michael had risen above just receiving the information. He now recognized he needed to make these answers work for him. He needed to develop his own process of putting all of this together for himself. Just as all of his mentors had created the answer that worked for them, he now understood it was up to him to make his answers, his process work for Michael.

He began to rethink all that he had learned from each person he had sought out. There seemed to be a statement, a process that had been created.

First, there was Specs Ifics. His message was: State the problem specifically.

The Guru Seeka Ansura embedded the importance of: Observe the problem resolved.

Then there was Mandrake, aside from all the smoke and mirrors, he suggested the key to success was to: List exceptions.

Dr. Structure's planned approach to dealing with problems was: Verify the plan.

Who could ever forget Buzz Nike's emphatic focus on: Execute . . . Just Do It!

During his sleep while his mind had been emptied of all this new input, Michael had made a startling discovery. He could envision a process that he believed would provide him with a resolution to his problems. He now understood the importance of his seeking out the information he had now acquired. His entire journey had been necessary in order that he could make his own self-discovery. At the end of the day, he had figured it out. He had figured out that he could now *solve* the same problems that had so paralyzed him. The process he needed to follow was:

S—State the problem specifically
O—Observe the problem resolved
L—List exceptions
V—Verify the plan
E—Execute . . . Just do it!

It had been there all this time. Now that he had discovered it, he began to give some thought to each part of the process. Michael wanted to make sure he understood each segment fully so he could feel comfortable in translating the process into action.

CHAPTER 7

THE SOLVE PROCESS

Michael truly believed that using the SOLVE process would empower him to coach himself to solutions. By adhering to these five steps:

> S—State the problem specifically
> O—Observe the problem resolved
> L—List exceptions
> V—Verify the plan
> E—Execute . . . Just do it!

Michael was now convinced that any problem could be SOLVEd. The question for Michael was no longer whether he could deal with new and different problem issues; it was rather how he was going to reSOLVE them when they developed. Now he knew, and more importantly than knowing, now he was able to do the SOLVEing that would provide him with ongoing solutions.

Here he was at the end of the day. Michael's concluding thoughts were really beginning thoughts. True, this was the conclusion of his journey, but in every other way, it was the beginning of how he would deal with future workplace and personal problems in his life. He was now able to SOLVE his way through them.

Change! That is what SOLVEing promotes. Michael's workplace environment had changed. Reengineered, rightsized, reorganized, or whatever the term, the end result was identical. Change! As his workplace surroundings changed, he needed to change as well. Problem issues that were someone else's were now his. People who used to help solve his problems were no longer there. It was now up to Michael, and that was the good news.

What an opportunity. Michael's self-potential had been given permission to be unleashed. His creative juices, his ability to initiate needed to be summoned. His personal challenge to become more productive had been issued. The ability to SOLVE his own problems had moved from being a luxury to becoming a necessity. All successes counted! What he did successfully in his personal life needed to be understood and transferred to his work environment and vice versa.

The SOLVE process allowed this to take place. The ability to see his successful self in the "bigger picture" needed to occur. It was being able to understand the process of his personal success that broadened Michael's ability to coach himself through problem situations no matter how or where they developed.

The SOLVE process had helped identify that Michael had specific problems that needed to be stated as such. By doing so, he was able to observe his problems resolved, which became the goal he wanted to attain. To help get started in achieving his identified objective, he needed to think about the times in his life when he had already lived the solution he was now seeking. These were listed as exceptions. Using these exception experiences as a base, he then developed a specific plan to once again achieve success in his life. Once his plan had been established, Michael needed to most importantly execute it, make it happen.

This process had developed into the SOLVE format that Michael had discovered. This made it possible for him to understand how to always be able to SOLVE not only his existing problems but future workplace and personal problem issues as well. Now that he knew how to SOLVE his existing problem issues he could never again not know.

Sure, he only had three months to SOLVE his problems at Ajax, but Michael knew that was going to be enough time to get it done. He had his plan, and he was ready to *just do it*! As for his relationship with Kim, he felt the most confident and optimistic about a successful outcome than ever before. Not only was he going to make his relationship with Kim work, Michael was excited about actually enjoying the process.

Michael now owned the ability that self-empowered him to face his future life issues in a new more confident, self-assured way. Michael had done it. *At the end of the day*, Michael had successfully completed his personal journey.

Dr. Ron Muchnick Ph.D. has over thirty years of sales, marketing, managerial, and motivational experience. He has a diversified operations and business background working in executive positions of major corporations, owning his own beverage distribution company and growing a large clinical practice (Counseling Solutions). The blending of these various perspectives and talents has allowed Dr. Muchnick to become an innovator in developing creative organizational environments. Doc Ron is the founder of Solution Focus Consulting and specializes in executive coaching, achieving personal excellence, team building, and sales and marketing innovations. He has taught a wide variety of courses for various colleges and universities and has been clinical director for Capella University. His academic degrees are numerous including an MA in marketing, an MS, and a PhD in marriage and family therapy. Doc Ron is a licensed marriage and family therapist in Florida and California where he now resides and is co-owner of the Counseling Center.

AT THE END OF THE DAY SEMINARS,
WORKSHOPS AND SPEAKING ENGAGEMENTS

FOR ALL INQUIRIES PLEASE E-MAIL TEXT OR
CALL:

E-MAIL: DOCRMUNCH@AOL.COM

PHONE/TEXT 858-886-6088
WEBSITE: www.SOLVEmodel.com

DR. RON MUCHNICK
3710 RUETTE SAN RAPHAEL
SAN DIEGO CA 92130

CPSIA information can be obtained
at www.ICGtesting.com
Printed in the USA
FSHW011946190519
58277FS

9 781643 50985